Forew...

Walking along a Devonshire lane before an 'Any Questions' programme with my old friend Tom Salmon the Manager of the BBC in Plymouth, I told him about this book and how difficult it was for me to capture the magic that was Caroline. The following week I received a letter from him; this is part of what he wrote:

'Her quality was, I think, to do with natural giving, as if she was blessed with some kind of cornucopia denied to lesser people and from it she dispensed kindness, care, concern and in your case, love, without the capacity for all these things ever being diminished within herself.

'Like those clear mountain lakes from which water cascades and the level never lessens she too, was fed by some unseen stream.'

That, indeed, was Caroline.
This was us.

David Jacobs

One

Some months ago, I went back to Spain. I took the same coast road from Málaga to Fuengirola and stopped at the place where the accident happened. I just wanted to feel close to her again.

It was dark when I got there. I began to feel apprehensive, just as I had that first time we went away together, and I watched her from a distance, waiting for me in her black coat, a silk headscarf covering her hair.

I stood by the roadside against a crumbling stone wall that marks the spot. A chilly, Mediterranean breeze blew through the darkness from the sea.

I closed my eyes and I saw it happening again: the car catapulting through the air; Dick beside me, rising from his seat in slow motion, his tanned face turning the colour of ash.

Then I saw her hair, spread out across the back of the seat, framing her face, just as it always did when she fell asleep.

Suddenly a car's headlights hit me, and I opened my eyes as they fled into the night. The wind died away and, for that moment, the road was silent. There was nothing there for me. I would never go back.

I can find her, though. She exists in my mind.

Her hair was always special to me. It was long and thick and golden in colour. I had dreamed about hair like that, lying beside me on a pillow, framing a girl's face.

She stood alone in the corner of London Weekend Television's hospitality room. The rest of the room was full of bustle. Charlton Heston loped about, looking for a phone to call his wife, while the unmistakable voice of a well-known cookery expert rose above the din of a production team, making the final preparations for recording 'Sunday Night with David Jacobs'.

She was an outsider, a friend of someone on the show. She wore a black dress and a little string of pearls, and she looked young and shy. Our researcher, a girl called Tanya, went over to her with a drink.

I couldn't take my eyes off that hair.

'Why don't you all come back to my house afterwards and watch the show,' I offered and, turning to Tanya, 'I hope you'll bring your friend.'

'Thanks,' she said. 'Her name is Caroline.'

'I like your house,' Caroline told me. 'It feels like a home.'

I stared at her. It was as if she already understood me. Home was what I valued most. Wherever I went, I always looked forward to getting back to a family life.

I had always been possessive about houses I had lived in. I usually overspent on them, too, and this one was no exception. It was a double-fronted, neo-Georgian house in Ilchester Place, which backed on to Holland Park in London. It had cost a small fortune, and my wife Pat had lavished a further fortune out of my income decorating the nine bedrooms, five bathrooms, four reception rooms and the rest. It was excessively elegant and smart, but it lacked the warmth of home.

8

Pat and I had little left between us. We no longer shared love, so the emptiness in our life had been filled with blame and recriminations. We had been married for twenty-three years, and, for what now seems like an eternity, I had been trying to find a way out.

I had often threatened to leave. I had even made plans to go. What stopped me were my four children and my home. Every stick of furniture, each painting, every single book represented the life which Pat and I had built together. I belonged to it all, just as much as it belonged to me.

I was forty-two years old, and I had been a husband and father for almost half my life. I was in the mould, and the mould had set. I was well and truly a family man. I could not bring myself to walk out on all I had worked for. Everything I stood for was in that house.

Caroline seemed to understand. She had called it a home. I looked at her.

'I'm going to marry you,' I thought.

I had the house to myself that evening. Pat was away with Joanna and Emma. Carol, the eldest, was staying with friends. and although my son Jeremy was around, he was out.

Caroline sat on the green sofa. A painting of a mother breast-feeding her child hung on the wall behind her. We had drinks and settled down to watch the recording on television.

Afterwards, as everyone began gathering up their things, preparing to leave, I said, 'Incidentally, I'm throwing a party tomorrow night. You're all invited.'

They all looked surprised. In fact the idea had only just occurred to me. It would be my first gesture to Caroline. It was a way of seeing her again.

'I hope you'll come,' I said to her. 'Bring a boyfriend, if you like.'

I spent the rest of that night and the next day worrying about whether she would.

The discothèque was a bizarre place. It had just opened off Oxford Street, and the décor was desert island. There were imitation palm trees, straw-roofed huts and flaming torches on the walls. Bodies crowded together on a tiny dance floor and gyrated under flashing, multi-coloured lights.

Our table for fourteen was beside a heart-shaped swimming pool. Gradually, the guests began to arrive. There was David Bell, the producer-director of my show, Peter Evans, the journalist, and his wife; and Elton John's manager, John Reid, who was then a young record plugger. Researchers and production assistants on the show came, too.

Caroline was certain to be late. I wanted her to come so much that she was bound to keep me waiting.

She arrived last, with her friend, Tanya Bruce-Lockhart, and, directly she walked in the door, I leapt up and elbowed my way through the crowd to meet her.

As she sat down next to me, she said, 'I thought perhaps your son might have come.' Jeremy was sixteen at the time.

'Oh, Lord,' I thought. 'She thinks I invited her for him.'

It was a carefree evening. Several of the guests stripped down to their underwear and plunged into the swimming pool. We drank only champagne. It was so impressive that I didn't mention to Caroline that I wouldn't actually be footing the bill. The management had given me £100 worth of credit to introduce some friends to their new club, which was one of the perks of the job.

Caroline was twenty-three. She wore a white lace trouser suit, which she had bought for her twenty-first birthday party.

I wanted to know everything about her. She had grown up in the country, though not the simple, rural kind. Her childhood home was in Pinkneys Green, which now lies just off the M4 motorway in the depth of the stockbroker belt of Berkshire. In countryside like that even the trees, fields and cows have a well-scrubbed, clean look, as if the wealth of the people who live there has rubbed off on nature.

Caroline's father, Johnny Munro, had exchanged the uniform of a captain in the Royal Artillery, with the unfamiliar wings that marked him out as a spotter pilot and the ribbons that showed him to have served in the Burma campaign, for the traditional city suit and the seemingly equally traditional daily journey to and from town: a journey and a routine that he longed to give up.

Caroline was an only child; Yvonne Munro had died when her daughter was fourteen. Caroline talked of her mother as a striking woman with dark, gypsy-like looks. It was she who had furnished their home with chintz curtains and velvet covers, pieces of polished silver, porcelain, bone china and four-poster beds.

I thought of my own children: like most teenagers, they often seemed set on being everything Pat and I were not. This was 1969: Caroline had grown up in the sixties, but that era of change hadn't touched her. She reminded me of girls from my own youth, who did what was expected of them. She didn't want to be different from her parents. She wanted to be part of their unchanging, respectable way of life.

On the day I had met her at the television studios, she had arrived in London from Cornwall, where her father had moved with his second wife. She had got off the train at Paddington station with nineteen pound notes folded in her handbag, to look for a flat, a job and, no doubt, someone to love. Meanwhile, she was sleeping on a sofa at Tanya's flat.

'My father never gives me too much money. He says I'll only spend it on nail varnish if he does.'

Although she was a tall girl, slightly taller than I, her hands were small and delicate and it was a family joke that she was always painting her fingernails.

This was her second attempt to find what she was looking for in London. Before the summer of 1969, she lived in Belgravia and worked as a production assistant for London Weekend Television. She had given that up and gone home when her first love affair ended.

The young man had lived in a penthouse on the opposite side of her street from where, one morning, he had spotted Caroline on her way to work.

She had met his parents at their large, country house, complete with dogs, a lake and a shoot. The marriage would have fulfilled all her father's expectations of her, and, being an old-fashioned girl in love, Caroline had assumed the young man would marry her. But, somehow, he never got round to it. When her phone stopped ringing, she stood at her window, watching his flat, unable to understand what had gone wrong. She clung to her idea of love.

One night, she looked out, and in the penthouse opposite, she saw another girl, framed in the window. Caroline had gone back home for three months.

It had been a hot summer. Now a mellow September had arrived, and she had come back.

Caroline and I began to dance to Stevie Wonder's 'Ma Cherie Amour'. We held each other in the old-fashioned way. As I watched the coloured lights flicker through her hair, her body softened in my arms.

Tanya was watching us. She was Caroline's closest friend, an intense and caring girl. Later, she caught hold of my arm.

'Don't hurt her, will you?'

Caroline was returning to Cornwall. She had found herself a place in a South Kensington flat, sharing with two other girls for £7 a week, but she couldn't move in for another three weeks.

By coincidence, I had to open a supermarket later that same week at Helston, which was just a few miles from the village of Helford, where her father lived. So I asked Caroline to meet me there.

I didn't press it. I kept the invitation casual. Instinct told me not to rush a girl like that, but it was hard. I had a great need to feel loved again. I had felt cold inside for a long time.

The night before I was to be in Helston, I was in Leicester to compère a cabaret, and I drove back to London to catch the night sleeper. The Cornwall express was just about to pull out as I rushed down the platform and flung myself into a carriage. I stood in the corridor, totally out of breath. It seemed like an omen for the day: I felt sure Caroline wouldn't turn up.

I was exhausted, but I couldn't sleep. Each time I closed my eyes, I saw her face.

A woman taxi driver met me off the train and took me to my hotel. She spoke about her son, a policeman in Kent, who returned each year to lead the Helston Furry Dance. I stared out of the car window, trying to spot Caroline. This was the town where she came to shop.

The hotel was a dreary place with heavy, dark oak-stained furniture and gaudy candlewick bedspreads in the room where I changed my clothes.

I studied my haggard face in the bathroom mirror as I shaved. At times like that, I looked my age. It was just as well she wasn't going to be there.

I was, however, still that recognizable face off the telly, a product of the national obsession with pop music. I was the man who rubbed shoulders with the Beatles, and at a country house we once owned at Angmering a high fence had to be erected to stop the more enthusiastic fans picnicking on the lawn.

Yet the turn-out at Helston was still a surprise. It was one of the biggest I had had. The main street was blocked with shoppers. Police had to divert traffic while I opened the store and the first hundred customers collected their free chickens.

Housewives in headscarves, loaded with shopping, perched their children on their shoulders to get a better look and pressed towards me as two big policemen elbowed out a path.

Faces in the distance smiled and called my name. Those who got close became curiously silent and shy, so I grabbed hands, asking people how they were and how they were doing, and feeling absolutely fine myself.

I was glad that I had convinced myself that she wouldn't turn up. Now I began to feel perhaps she might.

I stood with my back pressed against the meat counter, handing out autographs to eager, outstretched hands. I scribbled messages on shopping lists, cornflake boxes, even loo rolls and anything else that was to hand. As fast as I signed one, something else was thrust in my face.

I felt a tap on my shoulder. 'Hello, poppet,' said a voice.

What a strange expression! I hadn't heard that one since the war.

I wheeled round and there she was.

Caroline and I lunched together in a small Cornish restaurant of oak beams and thick oak tables, with linen napkins, silver tableware and sparkling cut glass. We sat opposite each other. We both had cold lobster, and the wine was Chablis, nicely chilled and very expensive.

'Flash Jacobs is certainly doing his stuff,' I thought to myself. It had been a profitable morning, so what the heck?

The wine was perfect, the lobster perhaps the best I have ever tasted. I looked across the table at Caroline.

She sat there in a yellow shirt and yellow slacks, with a blue belt that matched the colour of those ludicrously large eyes of hers. For the first time, we were alone together.

I said, 'You know, I don't think I've ever sat opposite such a beautiful creature as you.'

Caroline's face was a signpost. It showed everything she felt. At that moment it was anger: she was furious.

'I don't think I'm beautiful,' she replied. Even her voice was stiff. 'But even if I were, I'd hate to think that was the reason I'm being taken out to lunch.'

I don't know what reaction I had expected, but it wasn't that. What to say?

There was a pause, and then she laughed. 'You don't remember meeting me a long time ago?' she asked.

I shook my head.

'You walked into my office at London Weekend Television, clicking your fingers to a tune you hummed to yourself.'

I sounded dreadful. 'That couldn't have been me. Not unless I was fooling,' I replied.

'I don't think you were fooling,' she smiled.

An elderly man, whose name I still remember was Miles Wentworth Thomas, drove us to Truro station. He wore a black, belted mackintosh and a peaked driver's cap.

Caroline and I sat close together in the long, black car which wound sedately through the autumn lanes, while a pale, watery sun followed us. I couldn't stop looking at her.

I wanted Mr Thomas to drive even slower. I couldn't bear the thought of catching my train back to London.

Caroline and I hugged each other on the platform. She clung to me as the train pulled in, as if it was a real parting. I hung out of the window until she had vanished.

Then I sat back and thought about her. I imagined her as middle-aged, standing on a station somewhere, waiting for me. She would be plumper and more contented and wearing a camel-haired coat, but there would still be that long, golden hair that brushed my cheeks when I took her in my arms.

I woke with her face still in my mind.

Two

I arrived at Paddington station at my usual time. It was the same each Thursday. As I walked across the forecourt, the electric clock clicked to 12.35, which left ten minutes before I caught the 12.45 to Bristol Temple Mead.

The station was its uncrowded, mid-day self. Clusters of people stood near the barriers, staring up at the departures board, or past the platforms into the distant blackness, from which arriving trains emerged. Porters lounged against yellow trolleys, puffing crumpled cigarettes, while a few late travellers hurried past.

I walked across to the bookstand to buy my *News* and *Standard*, half listening to a loudspeaker voice, announcing delays. The sound echoed round the station arches and hung in the chill railway air.

Caroline was waiting halfway down platform 4. I stood at the barrier and closed my eyes. I opened them again, and she was still there in her black coat and silk headscarf.

Why on earth had she covered her hair with that blasted scarf? I passed girls looking just like that every day in Knightsbridge and South Kensington and never gave them a second glance. They even folded the damn things on their heads in same way. She probably had a copy of *Tatler* or *Country Life* under her arm as well.

What was I doing there? At that moment I felt like turning on my heels and running for my life.

Of course, I knew she would be there. I had woken that morning with my stomach churning at the thought. It had been madness to suggest meeting a young girl like that so openly. I never went anywhere in London without running into someone I knew.

I couldn't think what had possessed me. I had enough problems at home without being spotted with her. What made it worse was the thought that she almost shouldn't have been there at all. I nearly hadn't asked her to come.

I had written her a letter, suggesting dinner on the night after she arrived back in London from Cornwall. I explained that the only problem was that I would have to take her to Bristol to eat, as I had to be there to record my weekly radio programme, 'Any Answers'.

I wrote:

My hands are trembling at the mere thought of what you'll be saying to yourself. But assuming you will accept, I have already reserved two rooms at the local hotel. After dinner, I will take you to the door of your hotel room, which will be no different from me taking you to the door of your flat.

I wrote the words easily enough. But when I read them back, I couldn't even believe them myself. I decided not to send the letter.

Nearly two weeks had passed since that day at the Helston supermarket. I remembered the warmth of her breath as we hugged each other on the station platform, and then I went out, bought a stamp for the letter and stuck it on. But I hadn't posted it: I put it in my pocket and carried it around for a day or two, giving it some more thought.

Then I had bumped into Tanya at the television studios

the day before I was due to go to Bristol. She told me Caroline was at her flat. I couldn't resist any longer. I fumbled in my pocket for the letter and handed it to Tanya. She regarded me warily; she kept such a protective eye on Caroline. We had nicknamed her 'P.C. 49'.

She had phoned when she got my letter and had asked to see me. She was in a state when I arrived at Tanya's flat. She couldn't sit down. She paced about the room. Those small, delicate hands moved in sharp, tense gestures, as she puffed hard on a cigarette.

'I've decided to come to Bristol,' she announced.

'Oh, good,' I muttered.

'But I must ask you not to fool around with me. I'm not that sort of girl. I couldn't stand it.'

'Of course I won't,' I replied. I meant it, but she had still given me a shock.

Now I looked down the platform. Caroline still hadn't spotted me; she was staring across the railway track. The urge to run was overwhelming. The usual platitudes flooded my mind. I didn't want to ruin such a young life . . . she couldn't see the complications of getting involved with a man like me . . . she'd be better off in the end . . . and so on. . . . But I couldn't run. I had to get on that train. I had to do a programme for the BBC.

The train was almost due. I decided the only way was to ignore her, walk past her on the platform as if she didn't exist. I could explain my reasons later.

In those days, I always had the uncomfortable feeling that everyone recognized my face. The straggle of passengers who waited for the train glanced at me as I passed. I could almost see them mouthing my name and thinking, 'There's David Jacobs. What's he up to?'

I started to walk down the platform: I had almost reached Caroline. I prepared myself to walk hastily past when she turned and saw me.

She smiled. It was a tight little smile. She looked even

more scared than I was. I imagined one of my daughters standing alone on that platform. I couldn't have walked past.

'Why, hello,' I said, terribly loudly. 'Fancy seeing you here.'

Caroline stared at me blankly. Then her expression changed to embarrassment and her eyes looked past me, trying to see for whom I was staging such an act.

The train arrived. Caroline and I stepped into a first-class compartment and sat opposite each other. An elderly man followed us and sank heavily into a corner seat at the other end of the carriage. He was a thick-set fellow with a ruddy face, a bushy, military moustache and a tweed jacket. A pair of large, bulging eyes examined Caroline and me.

'What a coincidence meeting you here,' I continued, half addressing the remark to our fellow traveller. 'So you're going to Bristol as well.'

Caroline muttered something, then gave a cough, which sounded rather like a laugh.

'Hmm,' grunted the man in the corner, and disappeared behind his copy of *The Times*.

The train began to pull out. It emerged slowly from the station gloom, chugged past London roof-tops and gathered speed through the endless rows of suburban semi-detacheds, then burst into a patchwork of fields, wire fences and clumps of trees, lying quietly under a mellow sun.

Caroline took off her headscarf and shook her hair. The man in the corner lowered his paper and stared at her, and so did I. Each mile was taking me further away from discovery, and I began to think this hadn't been such a bad idea after all.

Caroline opened a copy of *Tatler*. She handed me *Country Life*. I remember reading about a stud farm which was being advertised for sale. It was in Wiltshire, and the photograph showed a wisteria-clad Georgian house. It had a drive of 375 yards, 26 loose boxes and a swimming pool.

I gazed out of the train window. The rusts, reds and golds of an autumn countryside stretched out around me. I imagined myself walking up that drive through tall, elegant trees as evening fell, saying good night to my horses, then going back to a house where Caroline waited for me.

The train reached full speed. It rattled along. Our fellow traveller began to breathe evenly and deeply. The newspaper collapsed slowly on to his lap as he disappeared into sleep.

I moved across the carriage to sit beside Caroline. We did the *Standard* crossword together, holding hands.

The BBC had sent a driver to Bristol station to meet me. The high, city buildings and people, bustling along the pavements, closed in on me again. The driver was young, but I guessed he was a family man. His thick pullover had the appearance of being knitted by a wife.

'By great coincidence, I met this young lady at the station. She's a friend of ours from London, who also happens to be staying at the same hotel,' I explained.

'Oh, yes, sir,' replied the driver, as he pulled up at some traffic lights. I watched his eyes in the driving mirror for a reaction. They followed the progress on the pavement opposite of a blonde in an extremely short skirt.

Caroline and I booked in side by side, but separately, at the hotel. I went up to my room and shut the door with relief, thankful to feel safe at last.

I began to unpack. This was easy, as I had only one change of clothes and I always packed neatly. But as I did so, I began to feel another kind of guilt.

For a man who can so easily spend every penny he earns, I had odd, unaccountable moments of economy, which I often regretted afterwards. I occupied my usual room, which in hotel language was called a 'superior single', which meant it was a large room with a double bed and bathroom. I had, however, economized on Caroline's accommodation. She had an ordinary single.

Now, it seemed a ridiculous economy. She was such a sweet, lovely girl, so well-mannered and nicely brought up, and the saving in itself was trivial. I picked up the phone and asked for her room number.

'Hello,' I said. 'Everything okay?'

'Yes, fine,' she replied cheerfully. Well, that, at least, was a relief.

'Come to my room for a drink,' I said.

She walked in the door and into my arms. It was the first time I had kissed her.

'Thank goodness I've got that over with,' I said. It had been a kiss of promise.

We had dinner. We held hands as we walked beside the dark river, twinkling under the city lights.

'I think I'm falling in love with you.'

'You can't be; it's not possible. It's too soon. I wish you hadn't said that.' Her voice was almost angry again, as if I were using the oldest cliché in the book.

We talked together in my hotel room. We sat in two armchairs, sipping whisky, the bed behind us.

'Look,' I said, when it had grown late, 'I really must get some sleep. But I don't want you to go.'

'I'm not sleeping with you,' she replied quickly.

'I don't expect that,' I said. 'All I want is to be close to you. We don't even have to get under the bedcovers. We could just lie on top of the bed. We'd be together.'

She stared at me. 'Go back to your room and decide,' I continued. 'If you don't come back, I'll understand.'

She got up silently and went. I dashed into the bathroom. I cleaned my teeth, squirted a breath freshener in my mouth, combed my hair and put on my dressing gown – a cotton one, as it happened. I wasn't really thinking like Noël Coward.

I lay on the bed and waited. The seconds turned into

minutes. All I heard was my own breathing. The hotel was still and quiet.

Then the door opened. Caroline stood there in her black coat, a white nightdress underneath. It was a frilly affair, with the frills in tiers, so that its shape resembled a Christmas tree.

She looked down at me, stretched out on the bed. 'My God, you're so sure of yourself,' she declared angrily.

I sat up. 'The trouble is, that's the last thing I am,' I replied.

She lay in my arms all night. I stroked her hair and her soft arms. We talked quietly to each other and, gradually, we fell asleep.

Her hair touched my cheek as I woke. I stared at her for a long time, looking at her face in the innocence of sleep.

Then I got out of bed and crept into the bathroom to straighten myself up. What did a young girl see in me? I had a small bald patch at the back of my head, and I didn't want her to notice it. I combed my hair carefully over it, brushed my teeth and gave my mouth another squirt of breath freshener. A few years earlier, I wouldn't have even cared about what I looked like when I woke up.

Caroline was awake when I returned to the bedroom. Those large, blue eyes regarded me as she sat with her head propped up by a pillow, her hair framing her face. We smiled at each other for a long moment.

'Why me?' she asked.

'I don't know,' I replied.

Three

A broadcaster's job is to sell himself and, like any sales-man, he spends a great deal of his life on the road. The spin-offs of fame are store and supermarket openings, personal appearances, cabarets and dinner dances, chats to ladies' luncheon clubs – and I did them all. Living up to what I earned meant I always needed the money, but it also meant being constantly away from home.

Even when life at home seemed unbearable, I was always homesick after two days away. I stared at my couple of suits hanging lifelessly in a hotel wardrobe and my solitary toothbrush in its mug, and I felt truly alone. It convinced me that I could only be a family man.

Night was the worst time, so I often found company in hotel bars, to put off the moment when I had to face a silent hotel room and a cold, unfamiliar bed. Once or twice I had come across men who, unlike me, had found that particular courage to walk out on their marriages. I remember them for the greyness of their complexions and the grubby collars on the shirts they wore.

We would have one drink too many, and then another, and as the night wore on, they spoke about their loneli-ness. They had made me thankful I still had a home where I belonged.

However, when Caroline came with me, I began

enjoying going away. She used to say that she went to all the best places – Scarborough, Scunthorpe, Skegness, and many more – which have now become just dots on the British map.

We travelled separately, booked into separate hotel rooms, as I was often accompanied by a TV or radio production team, and also there were all those people we might have bumped into who knew my wife.

Our deceptions were carefully planned. Caroline often posed as a newspaper reporter who had come to do an interview with me.

One afternoon, in a hotel bedroom in Skegness, I became her lover.

Later, as I drank with a crowd at the hotel bar, a page-boy handed me a note.

'How extraordinary!' I exclaimed to my dinner guests, as I pretended to read the note I had, in fact, written. 'A young friend of ours from London is staying at this hotel.

'She's a jewellery representative,' I contrived, 'up here delivering some family heirlooms to an old lady who lives in Skegness.

'Would you mind if she joins us for dinner?' I was becoming the perfect liar.

Caroline always waited until every light was out before she crept along the hotel corridors to my room, her white nightdress hitched up under the black coat. She stood in the doorway wearing the expression of a naughty child.

Once she shut the door, the room changed. If it was an anonymous, ugly hotel room, we didn't notice. Inside we were alone together. We felt complete.

Time was always short. We measured out moments together and each one was precious. We shared every thought.

Our moods changed like quicksilver. One moment we were silly, serious the next. I told her the corniest jokes, and she always threw back her head and laughed and laughed. Laughing together we drew close. There was such tenderness in her face as we made love.

She couldn't tell jokes. She stumbled over the words and ruined the punchline. 'Why can't I be as articulate as you?' she raged, pounding the bed furiously with clenched fists.

I grabbed her hands and started kissing them. 'Oh, darling,' she said. 'I want to be someone you're proud of.'

To make me laugh, she pulled funny faces and put on plummy school accents as she clowned about the room.

Once she caught me in the bathroom, combing my hair over my small, bald patch. She started to laugh, and I tried to join in, though I felt terrible that she had noticed it.

'Now you see what a middle-aged chap you're landed with,' I said.

I noticed my face in the mirror. It had gone quite red. Caroline was beside herself with laughter. 'I'll have to get a catalogue about wheelchairs so that I'll be ready for you,' she replied.

Then I started to laugh. I was really laughing.

'I've never been so relaxed with anyone in my life. I've never been able to say what I feel so honestly,' she used to tell me.

She talked a lot about loneliness. She had never been able to come to terms with her mother's death, and her father was a solitary man, wary of showing emotion : she had become the same.

When I told her that I loved her, all she had ever wanted to feel just poured out. 'David, please let it work. These past few weeks can't all turn out to be a waste of time – just something to put down as another piece of experience.

'If you and I are to be together – if it's meant – my one aim is to make you the happiest man possible. We'd set a perfect example.'

But we didn't set any kind of example in our secret world of endless hotel rooms. It couldn't work like that for long.

I had told Caroline shortly after I met her that my marriage was over and that I was in the process of leaving home. But as the weeks turned into months and I was still there, she began to doubt that I would ever leave.

She was so full of youthful hopes and impatience that it was hard for her to understand that I just couldn't walk out. However romantic it sounded, the house at Ilchester Place had to be sold, or at least Pat and I reach a settlement, which we were far from doing.

Divorce can be such a messy, painful business, and I wanted to avoid that. Even my lawyer had warned me to wait. All the capital I possessed was tied up in the house. I simply wasn't prepared to leave with just my clothes and a couple of chairs.

Caroline confronted me one night in a hotel room in Manchester. I had been compèring a cabaret and got back at about one o'clock. She had waited three hours for me, lying on the bed, smoking endless cigarettes. The room smelt like an ashtray.

I was always surprised that she turned up at all. All her past boyfriends had been nice, young fellows with sports cars and sports jackets. This was not my first experience of infidelity, but it was certainly hers.

'I've come all these miles to see you, and in the morning you'll be gone,' she said, much too quietly. 'This room has begun to close in on me. It feels like a cupboard. I can't stand always being hidden away. I've become frightened by what I'm doing. I know you've tried hard to reassure me, David, but I'm still unsure – of myself and you.'

I sat down beside her and took her hand. I knew what Caroline needed. It was a husband, a home, children, her own family to whom she could belong, as I belonged to mine.

'You're right,' I said. 'I shouldn't expect you to stand for this sort of life.'

Caroline gripped my hand. She was near to tears. 'So now you see I'm a weak, spineless child who, I'm afraid, loves you with all her heart.'

I took her in my arms. I stroked her hair. I assured her that I wanted to be with her always, but I was still a married man.

She pulled away from me. 'I've got to have some time alone to sort out what I'm going to do,' she said. 'And you've got to be absolutely positive, too.'

She stayed away for three days. Then she phoned me. We were back together, but the interlude had changed me. I had realized that the constant deceptions and dishonesty were wearing me down as well.

My whole life revolved around Caroline. She was my first thought on waking, my last when I went to bed. If I woke in the night, and I often did, I saw her face. The shape of a piece of furniture in the darkness made me imagine she was in the room.

I tossed and turned, thinking about her softness. She was the softest woman I have ever touched.

Each morning, I woke early and crept down the stairs to wake Caroline by phone from my study. Then we arranged how we could contrive to meet that day. When I went away, the arrangements were complicated enough, but in London it was even more of a nightmare.

The problem was that my office was the study at home. That meant I had to think up endless excuses to get out of the house. These deceptions were compounded by my secretary, Bridget Dryburg, who, in complete innocence and with her usual efficiency, entered each appointment in the leather-bound diary on my desk.

Caroline had just started work as a secretary to the deputy head of Cunards, the shipping line. She couldn't travel with me, except at week-ends. I had to see her mostly in London. If I couldn't make lunch, I met her after work at her office in St James's, and we snatched half an hour together while I drove her back to her flat.

The flat she shared in South Kensington was a dreary place, sparsely and badly furnished as cheaper, rented accommodation usually is. She tried to cheer it up with possessions from home, like little, heart-shaped silver bowls, jewel cases and porcelain dishes. There was a framed photograph of her mother, and cuddly toys from her childhood were on her bed.

The place still felt cold, so I bought her a rug. She liked to tell me that her family was connected to the Scottish Munro clan, so I got a rug with the Munro tartan on it. I wanted her to feel warm in bed.

She used to stretch out and touch the end of it with her toes. Funny, curly toes she had. She said that rug was the next best thing to sleeping with me.

Most evenings I stayed at home, ate my supper, watched television and worried about her. I was as uncertain as a boy with his first crush. What was she doing? I couldn't expect her to spend every evening alone. She was so young and lovely. I sat in my comfortable home obsessed with her half a mile away in that awful flat.

I was always writing notes to her. 'You write exquisitely. I keep all your letters and read them before I go to sleep,' she told me. So I would slip out at night and drop them through her letter box.

I often couldn't resist phoning as well.

'You are a romantic fool,' she said. 'No one has ever phoned me twice in an hour.'

In those days, we had a cairn called Shaggy who lived up to his name but also came in handy. Walking him at night was an excuse to get me out of the house.

I remember once, standing in a telephone box near Ilchester Place, Shaggy pulling impatiently on his lead while I dialled Tanya's number. Caroline was spending the evening with her.

A man's voice answered the phone. It was probably only Tanya's boyfriend, but I still panicked.

The voice at the other end yelled, 'Hey, Caroline, David Jacobs is on the phone, claiming he's a Mr Lewis, the man who repairs your television set.'

Most week-ends Caroline stayed with a married cousin in Berkshire while I remained at home. We needed the break. Like those thousands of other couples, caught up in the all-consuming strain of infidelity, the week-ends were the time when we had a rest.

Our first meeting after the three days' separation was in the downstairs bar at the Cavendish Hotel in Jermyn Street. It was our regular lunchtime place. We chose it because it was near Caroline's office in St James's Square. It also had the advantage of being darkly lit, and, as far as I could tell, no one I knew ever went there.

One day I arrived first as always. I sat down in our usual corner seat, just behind the door. The seats were black padded plastic with studs, and on the walls was a Regency-striped paper in a burgundy red and some Regency prints. There were wall lights, which were adjustable, so I turned mine away from my face.

Our normal waiter came straight across when he saw me. He was of the old school, a heavily built man with a bald head, who combined deference with familiarity as expertly as he mixed a martini cocktail.

He knew Caroline and me well. He didn't have to ask for our order. It was always the same : two scotches and two plates of chicken sandwiches. He probably guessed what was going on between the two of us, too, though with him we only ever talked about the weather.

I glanced around the room. No one appeared to notice me, so I opened the *Evening Standard*. It was almost too dark to read in the corner, but I never could concentrate anyway. Just staring at the pages gave me the appearance of having something to do.

One o'clock passed, and she still hadn't come. Then one-fifteen. I had stared at every damn page of that paper for half an hour. My eyes ached. I was angry and extremely unsettled.

This whole incident was typical of our relationship. The hours I wasted just hanging around for her! All my day planned round snatching just half an hour together, and then she couldn't even be on time.

She knew I hated waiting in public places. I felt every pair of eyes in the bar turn towards me. Through the gloom I thought I recognized a familiar face, but it was too dark to be sure.

The waiter hovered knowingly. I ordered a double and sank lower into the seat. She would have until half past one, and that would be that. I couldn't stand it any longer.

I downed my scotch rapidly. My stomach had started to churn. It was two minutes to half past. I signalled the waiter for the bill.

As he handed it to me, Caroline suddenly appeared in the door. She hurried over and sat down. Her face was flushed and agitated. Immediately, she lit a cigarette.

'What happened?' I whispered fiercely.

'My watch stopped. I didn't realize the time,' she said loudly. Why did she have to shout?

'Shh,' I hissed. I ordered another scotch. She couldn't eat anything and neither could I. We sat close together, our knees touching under the table. The room had settled down. Everyone concentrated again on their drinks.

'David, I have to tell you. I went back to Robert while we were apart. I spent the night with him.' Robert was the man in the penthouse.

It was a shock, but I had gone through too much in that last half an hour to really feel the impact.

'I don't blame you,' I replied. 'I don't want to ruin your life. Whatever you decide, I'll understand.'

She stared at me. She looked even more upset. 'But it didn't work with him. It never could now,' she said.

'You must be certain,' I continued. 'After all, he's got so much more to offer than I have.'

She was on the verge of tears. I couldn't take a scene as well. 'Come on,' I said, hastily. 'We can't talk properly here. We'll find a way of meeting later.'

I flung some cash on the table, grabbed her arm and hurried her out of the hotel and down some stone steps to an underground car park. It was a huge, cavernous place, and our footsteps resounded loudly on the concrete floor. There were only parked cars to hear.

'David, I tried to live without you, but I can't.' Caroline's voice echoed round the grey walls.

I hugged her. 'I'm going to Wales in a couple of days for the week-end. Will you come?' I asked.

'But you won't be able to feel the same about me. It will be different for you.' Anxiously, she watched my face.

'No, it won't. It doesn't matter. Just don't keep on about it. . . .'

I drove her back to the office and then returned home. I went straight to the bathroom and locked the door. As I turned the key I began to sob.

A few weeks passed while I made a decision. When I had finally made up my mind, I told Caroline. It happened that we were in Bristol, in the same hotel room where we had spent our first night together.

I told her at once. I wanted to prove I could get through that night and the next day alone with her, vithout going back on what I had said.

I explained that it was impossible for us to continue our relationship like this. The strains were too great. I was of no use to my family, to her, even to myself.

At home, I lived in a constant dream about Caroline. If someone spoke to me, I barely heard. I spent each day in a frenzy about seeing her, or in resentful, silent moods when I couldn't get out of the house. At night, my dreams repeated themselves into an endless nightmare. Caroline stood in a long, white dress and however hard I ran towards her, she remained far away.

My work suffered. Every day was planned around meeting Caroline. There wasn't much time left to concentrate on anything else. I couldn't sleep properly. The strain played havoc with my stomach as well.

Yet it was all for just a few sneaked hours with her. Our meetings were often tense, too. We used the preciously short time we had together to quarrel about my still being at home. And then I had to go home and worry about that.

It was no kind of life for Caroline, and to me it felt like a kind of dying. I was no longer myself. I was in no state to end my marriage, either. I had to be on my own, so I could find the strength to go through with a divorce.

I didn't want her involved in my marriage problems. The reason I had to leave home was because Pat and I had fought for years. I didn't want it to seem as if I was walking out just because I had found myself a young blonde.

I thought I had explained it well, but obviously I hadn't. Caroline was furious. I had never seen her so angry.

She accused me of many things. Of playing games with her, of never meaning any promise. I had ruined her life. Then her anger dissolved into tears, and I could cope with those. I knew that I would be able to carry through my decision.

She was quite brave that evening. Over and over, I promised it would only be a matter of weeks before we were back together. I would start looking for a flat. I would get down to all the things I never had time for when I was thinking up excuses to meet her. And in that way we managed to get through the night.

By morning, Caroline had begun to realize that I wasn't going to change my mind. There wasn't much time left together. We went down to Bristol Docks. It poured with rain, and Caroline couldn't stop crying.

The S.S. *Great Britain* was docked there. Her slim, black lines merged with a jet-black sky. We stood side by side, soaking in the rain, staring at the ship, and all the while Caroline sobbed. She was far too upset to go on board.

Then we caught the train back to London. She tried hard to control herself on the journey. She kept getting up and going out to the toilet to cry. Then she straightened herself up and came back, her eyes looking smaller and sadder each time.

I can see her clearly, getting into a taxi at Paddington station. As I sat down beside her, she began to weep. The cab passed Rutland Gate in Knightsbridge. In less than five minutes it would be outside her flat.

Caroline started to cry, just like a child.

'Oh, Mummy,' she cried. 'Mummy, help me.'

Caroline's mother had died unexpectedly, and it was a great shock to her. She had come home from school one day and found her dead. I could see a pale child with golden hair at a funeral; she had to be held up by her father as her mother's coffin passed.

Caroline felt her sudden loss deeply, and in her loneliest moments she always cried out to her mother.

I prayed that I could hold on to my decision.

The taxi stopped outside her flat. She got out, still sobbing. But the relief was intense when she had gone.

Four

The hardest part was not picking up the phone to dial her number. It would have taken just one call. I knew her number as well as I did my own name. Dialling it would have stopped all the hurting. But it would have hurt much more to leave home.

The house was full of telephones. I hadn't noticed before exactly how many extensions there were at home. There was temptation in almost every room.

I didn't even dare answer the phone at first, in case it was her. I was too vulnerable to cope with that. But I don't think she even tried to call me.

The deck was finally clear, and there was a certain relief in that. All the reasons I gave Caroline for our separation were true. But there was more besides.

I still couldn't really see myself leaving home. I couldn't imagine who I'd be or what I would become if I wasn't a family man. I had to give myself another chance to settle down again.

It took a great effort to shut Caroline out of my mind. I went out a lot. I even took myself shopping and bought a new raincoat, but that only made it worse.

Caroline was a great shopper. She was a Jaeger girl. She always wore classic, understated clothes, the kind her mother would have liked. But in dress shops she be-

37

came a different person. She would try on the most out-rageous outfits and swirl around the shop.

'Madam looks wonderful,' the sales lady would gush.

'Do you really think so?' Caroline would reply, in her plummiest voice.

She'd stare at herself in the mirror, fascinated by the different image. 'On second thoughts, I don't think it's quite me.'

Perhaps she wished it was. She was too shy to show herself off. She always settled for the plainest style in the shop.

I got my raincoat home and tried it on in front of the bedroom mirror. If only I could find out what Caroline thought.

I was never a trendy dresser. I wore the same con-servative styles for years, and even my small efforts to look different never appealed to Caroline. ('Dreadful' was how she described the turnback cuffs on my suits.) She liked me in casual clothes.

Pastel shirts, polo-neck sweaters and velvet trousers hung in my wardrobe, all of which she had gone with me to buy: each had become part of the times we had spent together. I shut the wardrobe door and hung my new mac somewhere else.

How often I wished that I could wake up one morning to find I had been divorced. If only it could have been as painless as that. Instead, I would wake up to her face still haunting my mind.

Slowly, I would look around the room. A line of soldier prints stared squarely down from the wall. The desk was by the window, in its usual place. All my clothes hung in a neat line behind louvred cupboard doors. Everything would be as it always was, and morn-ing showed it in a comforting, familiar light.

I slept alone in my dressing room at that time. I would listen to the sounds of the family, moving about the house: with the bedclothes around me, it felt so safe in bed. I was even thankful it was no longer necessary to creep down the stairs to phone Caroline. There was no deception about my life.

One day, Bridget arrived at ten o'clock as usual. We went straight into the study. It was a small room with white walls and bookshelves. Bridget typed at a pine desk, while I sat on a two-seater sofa to work.

I watched her dark head bent over the typewriter, her homely face lined with concentration. She was in her mid-thirties with a round, cuddly figure and three children of her own.

She knew me well, after all the hours we spent together in that small room. But it had never occurred to her that I was the unfaithful type.

David Bell, my producer-director, arrived. Tanya and another television researcher came as well, and they crowded into the study to plan that week's television show.

I knew Tanya must have seen Caroline. I tried to tell from her face how Caroline was. I was so afraid she might be ill.

Tanya smiled at me. Perhaps she, at least, understood the reasons for what I had done.

The meeting finished and Tanya gathered up her papers to leave with the rest. As she shook hands, I clung to hers as if it was Caroline's. I wanted Tanya to realize all I still felt.

When they had gone, I asked Bridget to bring more coffee. She left the study and I stared at the phone on the desk. Caroline's voice echoed inside me. She would be at her office. My hand reached for the receiver, I started to dial the number.

Then I hesitated. What could I tell her? Each morning, I glanced through the accommodation columns of *The Times*. Just the printed details about flats to let scared me. Each one sounded such a lonely place. I couldn't tell Caroline that was as far as I had got.

I only wanted to hear her voice. At least, I could find out if she was all right.

The pause was long enough. Bridget came back as I replaced the receiver. The phone rang sharply and she picked it up. It was someone confirming an engagement.

The room settled back to normal. The work routine started. There was always a large post bag to get through, as many as fifty letters a day.

I began to dictate a letter. I stumbled over the first sentence and Bridget glanced up. I repeated the sentence without a mistake. I felt in control of my life again.

My obsession with Caroline had inevitably made life worse at home. Her name hadn't been mentioned, and Pat hadn't even asked if there was anyone else. But I threatened to leave so frequently that even my wife had begun to take me at my word. Each time she returned after a few days away, she would say, in a tone of mock surprise: 'What, you still here! I quite expected you'd have gone by now.'

I felt as if I was living in my own home on borrowed time.

There were the children, but as they grew older, even they seemed to need me less and less. Sometimes I wondered if they needed me around at all.

Carol was a bright girl. She had passed three A levels by the age of seventeen and went on to get two more in a single year. At home, though, she was difficult. Her table manners were dreadful. She shovelled her food into her mouth with her fork and chewed loudly. I nagged her, but she never took any notice.

'Another Sunday lunch bites the dust,' Jeremy would say.

Carol had her own suite of rooms, which she kept in a disgusting state. Clothes hung out of every unclosed drawer. The rest was piled up in dirty heaps on the floor. She picked up nothing on principle, or so it seemed.

I had provided my children with a home that deserved

respect, and I warned Carol that if she didn't clear up her things I would throw the lot into the garden. She didn't. So I did, and I felt a lot better for it.

My father used to put me over his knee and wallop my bare bottom with a slipper. Excuses weren't listened to when I was a child. You either obeyed the rules or you knew what to expect.

I was strict with my children, but I tried to be fair. I could be persuaded to change my mind, but there were certain rules which were not to be broken.

Courtesy and good manners matter. A tidy home matters, too. We employed a cook, a cleaner and an au pair. Ilchester Place was a household of women. It should have been an orderly, well-run home.

Carol's untidiness was only a gesture of independence, but it was hard to see it like that at the time. It was constantly on my mind that I had failed the children by not making my marriage work, and any rebelliousness on their part seemed a result of an unsettled home. I tried hard to be a normal father, but it was difficult when nothing was right in my own life.

Jeremy was the only boy, and I always liked to imagine that he and I had a special relationship. We shared a joke about always knowing when the other was at home: we could tell because the loo seat was up.

We had been close when he was younger. We often went on boys' outings together. Sometimes it was a walk across Richmond Park and a bus ride home. Other times we took our bikes. A treat was a ride on the Underground. We took the Circle line and travelled right round it. The fun was that we only had to buy tickets for one stop.

At prep school, Jeremy had been captain of cricket, *victor ludorum* at sport and deputy head boy. He had seemed such a normal boy, until he arrived home from boarding school with an enormous shock of hair hiding his tiny face. He wore a fur coat, which he had bought off another boy for £1.

It was the start of the freaky look, and there were not many boys around looking like Jeremy. By adult standards the coat was frightful. The fur was raccoon or opossum, and it was full of holes. It was the sort of coat I would have used to cover the car radiator in winter, yet Jeremy wore it all the time. He spent hours getting himself ready to look terrible.

I held a black-tie party at a restaurant once, and he turned up in the fur coat and a waistcoat. He looked ludicrous. He wrote a letter, afterwards, apologizing for making such a fool of himself. It was a sweet, affectionate letter : Jeremy hadn't really changed that much.

He was always a sensitive boy. He was the one most affected by our marriage problems. Joanna and Emma were too young to be involved, and although Carol knew what was going on, she was clever enough to keep herself out of our problems. At sixteen, Jeremy was the one expected to take sides.

One night, after a row with Pat, I asked him if he would go and comfort his mother. When he refused, he broke down and wept. He cared for us both. He couldn't cope with the bitterness left between us.

Joanna was also transformed into an unrecognizable hippy when she went to Holland Park Comprehensive School. Her frizzed out, henna-ed hair, beads and Moroccan dresses didn't bother me much : by that time, I had learnt to swim with the tide. But when I heard she had been playing truant from school, I broke down. I wasn't crying for Joanna's failure, but Pat's and mine.

Jo wasn't wicked. When she broke rules she was always sorry. She hung round me, trying to find a way back into my life. Sometimes I would search for her in Holland Park, where she often sat playing the lute and smoking with her hippy friends. I'd take her hand

and we'd dance round the fountain together, singing songs. Jo needed me. She was a little girl lost.

Then there was Emma, who fortunately was not yet a problem. At eleven years old, she was still a typical schoolgirl in a tunic and high, white socks. Emma was still young enough to like doing what she was asked.

The days passed, and home settled down to how it was before there was Caroline. I tried to shut out thoughts of her by keeping myself endlessly busy. But the emptiness inside remained.

I had come alive in Caroline's arms, and I couldn't stop remembering that feeling. She had become so important to me that I had even found the courage to face her father.

Johnny Munro turned out to be an affable, generous man, nine years older than me. 'That idiot with false teeth and built-up shoes,' he used to call me in my 'Juke Box Jury' days. But we got on well.

We had gone for a drive together, when Caroline and I visited him in Cornwall.

He was fair-haired and blue-eyed, like his daughter. Every line of his features reminded me of her.

'I don't know what I'd say if a married man with four children was going out with one of my daughters,' I told him.

'Don't let's go into that. Let's just see what happens, eh?' he replied.

I poured out my loneliness in endless letters to Caroline. It helped to tell her all my thoughts. It felt as if I wrote each one down on paper. But I never did. I didn't send one letter; I just composed them in my head. I was still afraid she might have come rushing back, and I wasn't ready for that.

What was becoming clear, however, was that I had to do something. The chance I had given my marriage hadn't worked. And for her own sake Pat was pressuring me to leave home.

There had to be a trigger to make me accept that I couldn't give up Caroline, and that happened one morning, when I got out of a taxi in Curzon Street.

On the opposite side of the road, I spotted a girl in a silk headscarf and a black coat. My heart leapt. I could feel myself trembling as I rushed across the road and chased after that black coat. I overtook her and turned round, smiling absurdly as I looked at her face. It was a stranger's face. The girl stared blankly at me and walked past.

I had a consultancy job at RCA, the record company, and I returned slowly to the office. I was a man afraid of loneliness and at that moment I felt totally alone.

I picked up a copy of The Times. In the accommodation columns there was a flat to let in Park Lane. It was just around the corner. Slowly, I picked up the phone.

The flat was painted cream. Cream is such a boring, institutionalized colour. White would have been fresh and bright. The dark, mahogany furniture looked as if it had been lifted straight from those unmemorable suites in northern hotels. But the bathroom wasn't bad: it was tiled pink.

There were just two rooms, the bathroom and kitchen, but it was a reasonable price. With my other commitments at home, £35 a week was about all I could afford. The flat wasn't available for six weeks either. At least, I didn't have to move at once.

Now I really had some news for Caroline. Three weeks had passed since we had seen each other. She must have been wondering what on earth was going on.

She had to know at once; a letter would take too long. But I still hesitated about phoning. I had to consider those weeks to get through at home. I might change my mind again. Before I spoke to her, I had to be certain I could move into that flat.

I sent a telegram instead. After we had become lovers, that afternoon in Skegness, I had given her a silver figurine of an old man, dancing for joy on a plinth. The words inscribed underneath were: 'Skegness is so bracing'.

Caroline had nicknamed him Ambrose, so in the telegram I said:

GHOSTS BEING LAID HOURLY — AMBROSE, ALTHOUGH HIGH KICKING, IS PINING — HOPES VERY SOON TO BE RETURNED TO JOINT OWNERSHIP. MY LOVE FOR EVER. DAVID LEWIS. Lewis was a convenient pseudonym. It is, in fact, my middle name.

I was glad there was no reply. Caroline was a straightforward girl. She would have let me know if there was any change. Her silence told me she was still hanging on. It also gave me more time, and I still needed that.

I felt like a competitor in my own hurdle race. Each hurdle I overcame, I had to gather more strength to get over the next. The final one was moving into the flat. I would phone her directly I did it. I would have proved that I had left home on my own.

Three more weeks passed, and I coped a lot better knowing Caroline was still silently waiting for me. It was another Thursday. I arrived at Paddington station to catch the Bristol train.

Caroline knew I was always there at that time. It seemed her station. Somehow her train was the 12.45 to Bristol Temple Mead.

I walked briskly across the forecourt. I was thankful I had worn my new mac. The weather was fine and bright outside, but station air reduces any day to an unhealthy chill.

The faces I passed looked pale and bored. Once they had seemed to share my eagerness for the journey ahead as if they had someone like Caroline waiting at the other end of the line.

'The train standing at platform 4 . . .' That pompous loudspeaker voice had often struck me as funny, but now its discordant vowels grated inside my head.

A woman lugged a heavy suitcase across my path, so I almost tripped over it. People seldom looked where they were going. On the opposite side of the forecourt, I noticed someone running. Why couldn't people be on time?

It was a girl running. As she got nearer, I saw it was another of those girls in a black coat.

She'd had her hair cut. It was shorter, but not too short. She reached me and flung herself straight into my arms. I had never cared less whether there was anyone around to see us.

'You've bought a new mac!' Caroline exclaimed.

'You've had your hair cut!'

I couldn't stop hugging her. I could feel the warmth of her breath again, the touch of her hair on my cheeks.

'I had to come. I had to know whether you still want me to wait!' she cried. 'I've thought about you every Thursday, catching the 12.45.'

'And I've thought about you all the time,' I replied.

I had to let her go. I had to catch the train. Directly I arrived at Bristol Temple Mead, I phoned her. I always knew that once I saw her again I wouldn't be able to keep away.

If only, though, she had given me a little more time: I was still at home.

Five

I woke up in my dressing room at Ilchester Place on a Friday morning. It was April weather outside, crisp and showery. There was nothing to distinguish that particular morning from any other, except that I decided to leave home.

It was an impulsive decision. There was no need for me to go that soon. There were only nine days left before I moved into the new flat at 55 Park Lane, which I had taken on a three months' let. But I couldn't stand the waiting any longer.

Each day, some of my courage seeped away. I was afraid that, if I remained at home, I wouldn't have any left to help me go. Nine days more seemed unbearable when I had finally decided to walk out on twenty-three years of my life.

Caroline still doubted whether I would do it. She knew by heart every excuse for my remaining at home. There was always some family problem which needed me to sort it out. But that wouldn't work with her this time. I owed it to Caroline and myself to give life in the flat a chance.

Our six weeks' separation had changed nothing. In the two weeks we had been back together, our affair had resumed its intensity, with all the strain and sneaked meetings. But now I knew how hard it was without her. And Caroline expected more.

She wouldn't stand for it if I remained at home, and neither, it seemed, would Pat.

I guessed what was in Pat's mind. She wanted me to leave, to prove that I wouldn't be able to stand being away from home. She was certain that, sooner or later, I would come crawling back.

She probably knew about Caroline and thought my leaving home would be the best way to end our affair. It had happened before in our marriage.

My reputation with women was exaggerated. Mostly the relationships had been innocent ones. A woman's company has always appealed to me more than a man's. I would far rather spend an afternoon chatting to a woman than playing a round of golf or going for drinks with the boys.

I love a woman's softness. I have held a woman in my arms all night, without making love. That way, I didn't feel unfaithful.

On occasions, there had been more. Pat had discovered one affair and, after that, understandably had constant suspicions.

She knew me best. Sometimes I thought she knew me better than I did myself.

I got out of bed and went straight to my study to book a hotel. The White House off the Euston Road near Portland Place seemed unlikely enough for the press not to notice me there. The last thing Caroline and I needed were newspaper reporters chasing us around.

I couldn't wait to tell Caroline. Her voice on the phone sounded stunned. I gave her my hotel room number. That proved I really meant it, and I could hear how excited she had suddenly become.

I hurried upstairs to pack. Speed was necessary to my mood and also my schedule. In all other respects, this was a normal day, and I had to catch a train for that week's edition of 'Any Questions'.

I didn't bother to take many clothes. I could always come home for the rest when I moved into the flat. I packed some pictures of the children and a few books. Adventure stories, I think they were.

I went into the bathroom. Even with Caroline's company, I was still going to need some pills to get through the next week. I piled bottles of stomach settlers and sleeping tablets into the case. Emotion always goes straight to my stomach and gives me sleepless nights.

Caroline would be hurrying to work, full of hopes and plans. Everything I had promised her seemed about to come true.

'You'd leave home if you really loved me,' she'd often said. Now I was proving that I did.

Pat walked into the bathroom. 'So you're finally off,' she said dryly, glancing at the bottles of medicine and pill packets in the suitcase. 'Well, it's about time.'

Jeremy was in the hall, wearing his fur coat. He was just off to school.

'I'm going away for a few days,' I told him. 'I want to be by myself for a bit to sort things out.'

I wished that he knew Caroline. Then he might have understood why I had to leave him.

'Okay, dad,' he replied. He didn't seem surprised.

I parked the car at the station and took out my small overnight bag. It would be too late to return to London after the broadcast. I would have to wait until the next day to be with Caroline.

The other suitcases looked strange, piled up in the car like luggage for a family holiday. I slammed down the boot and headed for the train.

Often I had lain in Caroline's arms and planned this day, but I shouldn't have acted so hastily. I needed Caroline with me to reassure me that I had done the right thing. Now I had to face the first night alone.

Another man shared the compartment. He was a tallish

fellow, in his mid-thirties, who was probably feeling the first pangs of middle age. His ginger hair had started to thin even more than mine. To go with his colouring, he had a pasty face, but it was an open, friendly one.

He was reading a book about lawn growing, but when he felt my eyes on him, he glanced up.

'It's David Jacobs, isn't it?' He spoke hesitantly and blushed a bit. I nodded and smiled.

'My wife and I do enjoy your programmes.'

He probably had children, too. What would he have thought if he knew I had just walked out on mine? It crossed my mind to tell him. I wanted to see the effect on his well-meaning face.

I could have told him about Caroline's sweetness and warmth. Would he have envied me a girl like that?

He probably had a nice home. He wouldn't want to give it up.

I muttered something about doing 'Any Questions'. He looked impressed.

He would have been bound to tell his friends over a drink or two: 'Met David Jacobs on the train. Odd fellow. Told me he'd just left his wife. Swopped the 1949 model for a dishy '69 blonde.'

It sounded like a bar-room joke. Would I be judged like that?

The train ploughed through the countryside. Passing trees made stark outlines against a stormy sky. The earth looked cold and wet. Even the cows stood up.

'It looks like rain,' I said. My fellow traveller smiled. My public image was as a family man. I thought of all those newspaper photographs of me smiling at Pat; for years we'd pretended to be a happily married couple. This man still thought of me as a decent chap.

The panel on 'Any Questions' waited in a private room at the local hotel. It was a normal Friday. We sat down to dinner at 6.40 on the dot. At 8.25 I stepped on to the stage at the local village hall and introduced the audience to the panel of guests.

Caroline was listening to the radio at her flat. Apparently. I didn't even sound any different on the programme. Experience, I suppose, got me through. I had been on the radio since I was eighteen; I had been a broadcaster even longer than I had been a married man.

Drinks and sandwiches at the hotel followed the broadcast, and then it was time to be alone. A porter took me to my room.

I felt all right in other people's company. I wondered about offering him a drink, but there was none in the room. When he shut the door on me, I felt the whole weight of silence he had left behind.

It was raining hard outside. It hammered on the window of the room. It was the only sound.

I was desperate for Caroline. She was all the strength I had left. I picked up the phone and called her. She chatted excitedly about some kitchen utensils she'd dashed out to buy for the new flat. I couldn't ruin everything already. I had to stick it out.

I opened the case. I hadn't much in the world now. Most of it was in front of me, folded in neat little piles. My spare suit looked so cramped in there I nearly wept. I took out the sleeping pills.

I lay on the bed and imagined myself going home. Even in the dark, I knew where every stick of furniture was.

It didn't matter what other people thought of me when afterwards I could go home. It was the place where I could be myself. It was where I belonged.

At night, I bolted the front door and walked up the stairs past the rooms where the children slept. Sometimes, I stood outside their doors, listening to the rhythm of sleep. There was never the silence in a house that there was in a hotel room.

I wondered if Pat lay awake as well. We hadn't only had bad times together. We had had happiness from our children and our family life. What had I done to her?

If only I had never met Caroline. Infatuation always made me feel strong enough to do anything. But infatuation didn't last. It was easy for a young girl to make a fool of a middle-aged man.

Nothing was as secure as home. That never changed. That had always been there.

I should have been more like my father. From the moment he set eyes on my mother, there had never been anyone else.

I came from an ordinary, suburban home in Streatham where Mother and Father ruled the roost, and my brothers, Dudley and John, and I lined up in order of age to have our photographs taken. I had never known anyone who was divorced.

Even when I moved into the so-called sophisticated world of television it still gave me a shock to meet someone who had been married more than once.

Perhaps being Jewish had made me cling harder to the family circle than most. I remembered how I had tried to call off my marriage to Pat. I was only twenty-two. I wasn't sure of my feelings, but Mother was horrified. No one in the family had called a wedding off.

Even as a boy I wanted to become a family man. My parents were strict, but it was a loving home. There were always hugs and kisses between all of us. I never realized that my parents quarrelled; they kept their fights until the children had gone to bed.

My father had owned a fruit-importing business at Covent Garden, and we lived in quite a grand way. We owned a respectable house in Telford Avenue and kept a chauffeur and living-in maid. Then fruit supplies stopped when war broke out, and Dad went bankrupt. We moved into a small flat, where Mother started a home dressmaking business.

I remembered my sadness watching Father leave to tramp round shop after shop, trying to sell patent-leather gas-mask holders, which was Mother's latest fashion design.

Mother didn't see the sadness. She realized it was Father's way of restoring the family's pride, and he paid back all his creditors, though he broke his health and spirit doing it.

It wasn't a perfect marriage. Mother was a forceful, energetic woman, not above reminding Father she was used to better times. He wasn't easy, either. He was quiet and withdrawn, often moody. It upset him that he could no longer provide Mother with a comfortable life. But in their quiet moments they often sat holding hands. Their marriage was a partnership.

That was what I had wanted from mine.

Caroline gave me the chance to try again, but I was middle-aged. I was what my marriage had made me. It was too late to change.

Dick Marsh was returning to London by train, so I travelled with him. We had appeared on several radio programmes together, and, though I didn't know him well, I liked him instinctively. I had the feeling he shared some of the same problems as mine. That particular morning, Dick seemed more than usually withdrawn. He stared out of the train window, as if I didn't exist.

I felt I had to talk to someone. I had had all night alone with the panic I now felt.

'Dick!' I said. He turned slowly towards me, as if my voice came from far away.

'I don't know if I should be saying this to you. But I've got a feeling you'll understand. I did something terrible yesterday. I left my wife. In fact, my suitcases are in the car. It's parked at the station.'

Dick stared at me in disbelief.

'That's amazing,' he said. 'I've just done the same.'

Dick's face was as pale and strained as mine. But the coincidence was too much. Our expressions crumpled. We had to laugh.

Dick was a revelation. Sitting in front of me was proof that other men did what I had done. I began to think I would survive it. I even wondered why it had taken me so long to walk out. I was free, and suddenly it felt exhilarating. My life was honest at last. Even Caroline didn't have to be a secret.

'I won't exactly be alone,' I told Dick. 'I've got a sweet friend. She'll be coming round to see me a lot.'

'Oh, I'm glad for you,' Dick replied.

'Have you got anyone like that?' I asked.

'Yes, I have a friend, too.'

Now I had started talking, I couldn't stop. I told Dick everything. He was just as frank about his life.

The train drew into the station. 'You must both have dinner with us when we're settled,' I said. 'Nothing grand, I'm afraid. Just shepherd's pie on the kitchen table, I expect.'

'Shepherd's pie!' Dick exclaimed. 'My favourite food.'

'Splendid. I'll get Caroline to arrange it.'

'Caroline?'

'Yes,' I said. 'That's her name.'

'Good Lord, my friend's called Caroline, too.'

At the station we shook hands, and wrapped our arms around each other. We were friends.

We drove off in opposite directions: Dick took his suitcases to a new address, and I went with mine to the hotel room.

I have always been sensitive about hotel rooms. One

may be perfectly functional and clean, but I will still take an instant dislike to it. Perhaps the windows are too small. The room is dark or the colour of the walls will be one I can't stand. But mainly it's the feel of a room that I don't like. Sometimes I change hotel rooms twice, even three times, before one feels all right.

I changed my room three times directly I arrived at the White House. I ended up in one that felt more dreadful than the first. It was probably quite a respectable room, but each time I was alone, I panicked. I couldn't stand my own company for a moment.

Caroline rushed straight over. She burst into the room, her arms full of spring flowers. Her face looked a picture, and I felt ashamed of my own drawn, tired one.

'I'm going to learn to cook for you,' she declared, as if that made up for everything.

She had bought a cordon bleu cookery book. It was the first one of a series which was being published each week; there were seventy-one to go.

She held me. 'Darling twitface, everything will be different when you move into the flat. We'll be a perfect couple.'

She was right. Already I felt stronger in her arms.

I had gone this far for Caroline. Only eight more nights stood between our new life together.

All I had to do was to last out without going home.

Six

I did last out. I moved my suitcases into 55 Park Lane the following week-end.

Caroline was to cook our first Sunday lunch. She arrived, loaded with wooden spoons, mixing bowls, cookery books and goodness knows what. I showed her into the kitchen. It was a windowless room, not much larger than a cupboard, and she rushed around it, rifling through wall units, testing the cooker, grumbling all the while that there wasn't much to look at.

It was only just past eleven o'clock, but she seemed anxious to start lunch. She poured the contents of her basket on to a work-top. It was a narrow one. Potatoes rolled off and bounced around my feet. A bag of flour began to leak.

I picked up a potato. 'Leave it, David.'

I straightened up in astonishment. She had sounded just like a wife.

She smiled and put her arms around me. 'I'm sorry. But it's so small in here, I'll get on better if I'm alone. You go and do something else.'

It was difficult to know what to do in two rooms, kitchen and bathroom. I wandered into the bedroom and started to unpack.

Everything was mahogany, just like Maples' furniture shop in '58.

There was a crash from the kitchen. Caroline swore loudly. That sounded familiar. It began to feel more like home.

The living room was full of spring flowers which, once again, Caroline had provided for my arrival.

A sofa, a sideboard and two winged chairs faced me. There was a mahogany dining table and chairs as well. A nondescript painting of ducks flying into a sunset hung on the wall.

I placed some photographs of the children on the sideboard and stood on the balcony outside which looked across at Hyde Park. A spring sun had brought out some families, who strolled together across the grass.

Caroline had bought some Sunday newspapers, but there were so many divorce reports in the popular press: each one I read felt too close to home. I picked up *The Sunday Times* instead.

I soon put it down. I wasn't settled enough to read. The only subject I could concentrate on was myself.

What on earth was Caroline doing in the kitchen? It was past mid-day.

Even she had changed in the past week. I had never thought of her as my mistress. She had never been kept by me, though in one way it would have been easier if she had: I could have stayed at home and found her the flat. But she wasn't the type. She was far too proud for that. She wasn't a sensual woman, either. Making love to her was warmth and sweetness. Sex didn't really matter to her.

She was the marrying kind. That's what all those new kitchen utensils and cordon bleu books were about. Now I had left home, she had started to think of herself as almost a wife.

Didn't she realize that it was awful when she left me alone? At home there always seemed plenty to do. When the food was ready I just stopped what I was doing and sat down to eat. I had never waited around for a meal before. I hadn't realized how long one took to cook.

I decided to take a walk. I pulled on my overcoat. 'Just popping out,' I called.

'Okay.' Caroline's voice didn't sound concerned. All she was worried about was that damn joint.

I walked round the block. In front of me, a man pushed a pram. Its newness glinted in the sun. He was new to fatherhood, too. He kept peering inside to see if the child was all right.

I became a pram owner when Carol was born. I remembered how often I had pushed her around the park. I had been so proud of that pram.

The man with his pram disappeared round a corner. I started missing Caroline again. I headed back to the flat.

The entrance hall had a bright red carpet and two uniformed porters behind a desk. It looked such a swish place until I opened the front door of the flat.

Caroline had laid the dining table. She emerged from the kitchen, looking hot and dishevelled, but that hair of hers never looked a mess.

'Thank goodness you're back!' she cried. So she had missed me, too.

'I was afraid lunch would spoil,' she said.

The table had a new red cloth. A single red rose stood by my plate. She handed me a corkscrew and a bottle of claret. As always she had thought of everything.

Caroline watched nervously as I ate. There was avocado pear, roast beef and Yorkshire pudding, apple pie and whipped cream. I wouldn't survive many meals like that.

'Marvellous,' I murmured. 'Delicious. How did you manage it?'

She explained in great detail. I began to understand why it had taken so long. She had worried about the

Yorkshire pudding being flat. I nodded my head and munched my way through the lot.

I looked at my watch. It had taken nearly two hours to cook the meal. We had eaten it in twenty minutes flat. It seemed like an awful waste of time.

Caroline stretched her hand across the table and asked me if I had really enjoyed it. I looked into her anxious blue eyes. I handed her the rose beside my place and told her it was the best Sunday lunch I had ever had.

Next morning, I went shopping. I remember the strangeness of buying my first packet of tea bags. I no longer felt like a family man.

There were several reasons why Caroline didn't move into the flat: it was so small, and when she did stay the night, I always worried about one of the children unexpectedly turning up. But, mostly, it was because I didn't feel settled myself. I was by no means sure I could stand it there.

Those days at 55 Park Lane are memorable for their simple, unvaried routine. I was in the bathroom by 5.30 each morning. My stomach hadn't settled after the move, and neither had my spirits. The silence got me.

I had always been domesticated, but having so many daughters and staff at Ilchester Place, I hadn't lifted a finger around the house for years.

I reckoned, though, that I kept the flat as well as any woman. I never dusted round an ashtray or an ornament. I always picked it up and dusted underneath; more likely, I took the ornament into the kitchen and washed it as well.

I was never strong in the cooking department, but breakfast I could manage. Eggs and toast and tea bags in the pot were ready for Caroline's arrival each morning when she popped in on her way to work. For an hour at least our spirits were lifted.

We had only a few friends left. At Ilchester Place, Pat and I had entertained constantly, but most of the friends we had shared were out of the question, and Caroline hadn't lived in London long enough to know many people. But there was Dick Marsh and his Caroline.

They were our first dinner guests, and we did eat shepherd's pie. Dick also proved it was his favourite food. He took the leftovers for his breakfast the next morning.

Dick's Caroline was a lively, intelligent girl, who worked as a personal assistant to a political correspondent for the BBC. She was attractive, though not in a glamorous way. She had the look of a nice wife. She was the kind who said outrageously flirtatious things, but would have run a mile if a man had tried to take her up on any of them.

She and Dick were close and their relationship was also secret. Neither Dick nor I wanted to broadcast the fact that we had left our homes. What we also shared was the problem of a well-known face. We lived in a curious no-man's-land of going nowhere and seeing virtually no one, unless we were at work.

The two Carolines took to each other at once. They became great friends. Understandably, they had a lot in common. As they also shared the same name, my Caroline was nicknamed 'Charlie'.

It was a time when I desperately needed to be occupied, but too often I hung around the flat with nothing to do. My career had begun to suffer, not because my image had slipped, for few people knew I had left home. But I knew, and it was constantly on my mind. I couldn't concentrate as hard at work.

I had a weekly programme on television. It was a mid-week chat show, full of glitter and glamour, on which I talked to various guests, in between song-and-dance routines.

It went out at six o'clock in London. Viewers in the other regions watched their local newsround programmes for twenty minutes before tuning in to my show. By that time, it was well under way. The latecomers had no idea what was going on. It was a disastrous formula, but I had just accepted it. I felt so drained, I couldn't take on the battles to get the programme right.

Caroline tried so hard to make me settle in the flat. She practised her cooking – she was a natural cook – and she constantly bought me flowers.

I bought flowers, too. The florists' bills were astronomical. Apart from the photographs of the children, they were the only things in a flat of other people's furniture that seemed a part of me.

Caroline always rushed over when I got depressed. She spent hours talking to me or just holding me, as if I was a child.

'Give yourself time. It's not a bad flat,' she said.

She urged me to go out. She couldn't understand why I had made myself a virtual prisoner in the flat. But I was too afraid of meeting someone who knew Pat. I didn't want anyone to have a go at me for leaving her. I didn't even want to hear what was happening at home.

'Tell some of your friends,' Caroline said. 'They won't blame you.'

The only safe place was Caroline's arms. I became desperate when she had gone. I felt like rushing out into the street and shouting out that I was a chap who had left his children and his wife. Caroline didn't seem to understand there were too many people who would be hurt. Too many lives involved.

Pat might be right. I might have to go home.

Caroline became quieter as I grew more moody and withdrawn. She seemed at a loss to know how to help me, when we loved each other so completely.

My silences hurt her, but I didn't want to tell her the hopelessness I felt. I wrote her notes instead, to explain that I still wanted her, but it was so hard to accept that it seemingly meant losing everything else.

Caroline read the notes. 'Do you want to talk about it?' she asked.

'No,' I replied. 'The mood has past. I feel better now you're here.'

We avoided talking about the future. We seldom laughed.

Caroline arrived as usual one morning. She sat down at the table, poured herself some tea and buttered a slice of toast. Then she opened her copy of the *Daily Express* and turned straight to the 'William Hickey' gossip column. There was a long silence as she devoured it from end to end.

It irritated me. There was enough silence around when she wasn't there. She should have understood she was all the company I had left, how I had grown to hate everything about that flat.

'Can't you fill your head with something more important!' I exclaimed. I was feeling low. I had been up with my stomach in the night. She hadn't even bothered to ask how I felt.

'Why not try the leader column of *The Times*,' I continued. 'We might have something to discuss, instead of staring at the television all evening.'

Her mouth tightened. I had tasted that temper of hers recently. I had taken my daughter, Jo, to a Chinese restaurant and got back late, which made Caroline livid.

'Haven't I hung around for you enough already?'

She resented my past. Even sharing me with my children now seemed to make her jealous. She blamed the protectiveness towards my family on my Jewish nature. 'Unnatural' was the word she used. It didn't seem exclusively Jewish to me. Those who didn't need a family seemed the unnatural ones.

How could she judge? In the protected little world she had come from, she had never realized that she had known a Jew before, though her father had several Jewish friends.

I had thought Caroline perfection and that had been a mistake. I wondered if I had fallen in love too quickly. Sometimes she sounded so young.

Her body stiffened when she was in a rage. There was no softness left in her face. It became a tight little ball.

'Gossip columns tell me about friends of mine. People I used to know. People who still have a good time, instead of sitting around in a pokey flat with the bloody bore you've become,' she yelled. 'You're just fucking well jealous that I know these people. It gets you that I could be having a bloody good time.'

That was another thing that annoyed me about Caroline. She swore far too much. Swearing was something my father loathed. Though he mixed with hard, rough-talking men at Covent Garden, I had never heard him swear.

'Don't be so fucking annoying,' I told my mother once, when I was grown up. My father overheard and smashed me across the face.

Well-bred Caroline might be, but she could swear like a trooper.

I replied, as evenly as I could under the circumstances, that her friends were not the sort I would wish to know. Empty-headed people, whose means of expression is limited to expletives. Did she know what their solution to a serious problem like racial prejudice would be?

'Yes, flog those black buggers and kick out the Jews.' Caroline's eyes blazed at me.

There was silence. Caroline looked frightened.

With tears in her eyes she bolted for the door. I stood at the window and watched that black coat hurrying down Park Lane. The tears would have started to pour down her cheeks by now.

Caroline was a girl who needed to belong, and she had begun to feel that she didn't really belong in my life. But I didn't belong to myself, not in that flat.

Caroline wanted security, and now I had none left even to give myself.

My listlessness increased. I couldn't get into bed or out of it without taking a pill. I thought about those men I had met in hotel bars, with their grubby collars and their loneliness. I had left the shelter of home, too. I knew exactly how they had felt.

Caroline started going out alone. She took herself off for walks. Her solitary figure hurried across Park Lane and disappeared through the trees in the park.

The grass was covered with sunbathers. The sun blazed down. It had become a brilliant summer, but Caroline didn't seem to notice.

She was often gone for hours. I wondered if she would come back.

'Where did you go?' I asked.

'I just walked round the Serpentine. I must have done it several times.'

Neither of us was thinking straight any more.

Seven

A Saturday evening arrived, Caroline usually stayed at the flat at week-ends, so after we had watched all the television we could stand we went to bed. I had been away from home for exactly two and a half months.

We made love. Briefly, I found myself again in Caroline's arms. As she drew away from me, I reached for the bottle of sleeping tablets. One was no longer enough. I took a couple and lay back to wait for sleep.

Caroline stirred in the bed. A loud knock at the door had woken her. I rolled over and switched on the bedside light. It was ten past one. No one could be there at that time. We must have imagined it.

The knock sounded again. Caroline sat up and we stared at each other, trying to think who it could be. We knew no one in the block. It might be one of the children. They had all called to see me occasionally at the flat.

Whoever it was hammered at the door. Suddenly, I recognized that knock. I knew exactly who was outside.

'It's Pat,' I said.

Caroline's eyes widened. 'It can't be,' she whispered, pulling the bedclothes around her. Neither of us had anything on.

'Oh yes it is,' I replied. 'And she won't give up when she knows I'm inside.'

The panic started. 'Shall I hide?' Caroline asked. Her eyes searched the room. It was difficult to conceal someone in a small flat.

'The cupboard,' she said.

'That would probably be the first place Pat would look.'

I remembered the balcony outside the bedroom window. It ran right along the flat.

'You could wear your coat,' I told Caroline. 'You'd be all right out there until I've got rid of her.'

The knocker thundered again. All the neighbours must be awake by now.

I pulled myself together. There had been enough deceit. 'We can't start all that nonsense again,' I said. 'Sooner or later, you two have to meet. I've got to let her in.'

Caroline nodded, but she looked scared.

Pat stood outside in a long evening dress. Diamonds I had once bought her flashed on her ears and about her neck. It was a magnificent sight.

'I've just come from a party,' she said, pushing into the hall.

She handed me a brown-paper parcel, tied with string. 'Clean underclothes. You've been away so long, I thought you might be needing them.'

She stared over my shoulder at the half-opened bedroom door. I knew why she had come. She wanted to find out who had kept me away from home so long.

'There's someone here you'll have to meet,' I said.

Caroline appeared in the doorway. Her hair was newly brushed, her feet were bare. There wasn't a trace of make-up on her face. She had put on her coat.

'So you're the child who has taken my husband,' said Pat. My eyes felt like lead. Suddenly I remembered those two sleeping pills I had taken. How could I keep awake? I got both of them into the living room and sat them down. Pat and Caroline faced each other in the wing chairs. I took the sofa and poured myself a large brandy.

'I suppose you know all this has happened before?' Pat said.

Caroline looked terribly pale, but her voice was all right. 'David has told me everything,' she replied.

'Do you know about his nervous complaint – how he spends half his life in the bathroom?'

My head began to swim. The sleeping pills didn't like what was going on – particularly the brandy.

'I don't care about that. It doesn't matter,' said Caroline.

'You'll have to excuse me,' I said.

I didn't want to leave them together. But the bathroom was a necessity. Pat was right. At all the wrong times, my stomach did terrible things.

I got back to find them still talking. The subject was inevitably me. Pat explained how difficult I could be, and Caroline listened. I tried to add a word, but I didn't succeed. The most I managed was to stop myself from falling asleep.

Caroline told Pat her life story. She spoke of her loneliness when her mother died. She even apologized for taking me away from Pat. She had tried to live without me. But there could never be anyone else.

Pat looked touched. She explained the problems of being married to a man like me.

'You're so young,' she told Caroline. 'There would be someone else. But he's my husband, and he'll come back.'

I must have fallen asleep for a moment. The next thing someone was shaking my shoulder. It was Caroline.

'David,' she said loudly. 'Pat wants to go home. It's late. I want you to take her back.'

It was three o'clock in the morning.

I stared at her in astonishment. I couldn't believe she was asking me to do that. 'I'm in no fit state to drive,' I replied. 'Besides, I've got my dressing gown on.'

'David, please.'

If that's what she wanted, I'd get a taxi.

Pat and Caroline shook hands in the hall, while I struggled into my overcoat. For a moment I even thought they were going to kiss each other. Then Pat and I went down in the lift together. She seemed satisfied with her visit.

'She's a nice girl,' she said.

'Yes, she is,' I said.

'Will you be coming home for the rest of your things?'

'I don't know yet,' I replied.

Caroline was still in the living room when I returned. She was curled up in the chair. Her face looked so small and sad. I just couldn't help loving her.

'It's different now I know Pat,' she said quietly. 'She wasn't real to me before. She was "the wife", the woman I could blame for everything that had gone wrong in your life. Now I actually feel sorry for her.'

We stared at each other. I knew what she was going to tell me.

'David, I think you should go home.'

I was in no state to talk. We would have to discuss it in the morning. I had to get some sleep.

We did talk about it next morning, and each day of those two weeks left at the flat.

Going home had seemed inevitable even before Caroline had met Pat, and Caroline knew it. She urged me to return with a face that had grown thin with strain. I had never loved her more, and yet I had to try and give her up.

So I returned home. Caroline wanted it that way, and so did Pat.

Eight

'You shouldn't be here, Dad,' Joanna told me. 'We know you only came back because of us, but we're not children any more. We'll be all right.'

My marriage was over, but I had gone home to find that out. Only the prop of family life had held it together over the years, and I returned to find even that wasn't there any longer.

The children had adjusted to me not being around. Carol spent most of her time with three friends at a cottage at Fovant in Wiltshire, and shortly after I went back Jeremy left on a trip round the world. He never could stand being on his own with Pat and me.

Emma and Joanna were still at home, but they didn't spend much time there. They were becoming old enough to want their own lives. Soon they wouldn't need me at all.

'I can't spend the rest of my life trying to revive a dead marriage,' I told Caroline.

However hard we tried, Caroline and I never kept apart for long. Within weeks of my being back at Ilchester Place, we started meeting again. Even that hated Park Lane flat seemed a haven once I got home.

Caroline had no reason to trust me. She came back because she didn't have a choice. She was totally committed. We saw each other whenever we could. Caroline started to come away with me again. If Pat knew, she ignored it, for there was such a hopelessness about our marriage that even infidelity didn't matter any more. All that remained was to dismantle twenty-three years of our lives. We were finally discussing divorce.

The house was up for sale. The belongings of the marriage were to be divided. The children would share their time between both of us. It was as painful as I always knew it would be.

The hurt was so great that I suffered bouts of acute melancholia. I travelled through tunnels of blackness in my mind. But at the end of each tunnel Caroline waited. She had endless patience now she knew for sure she came first in my life.

The relief when it was over was so great that Pat and I parted in a civilized manner. The children had accepted the inevitable. Emma was nearly thirteen at the time, and for all the innocence in those hauntingly dark eyes of hers, she had always been a worldly child.

'Thank goodness,' she said, when I told her about the divorce. 'I've been expecting it for years.'

There was a 'sold' notice board in the front garden of Ilchester Place, and two removal vans waited outside. Pat and I had gone round the house together, and whatever furniture she wanted, I marked with a piece of chalk. It was like an auction sale, except I no longer cared what she took. I had Caroline. Too much time had been lost in our life together while I had been at home, reaching a divorce settlement with Pat.

One removal van took Pat's share of the furniture to a house she had bought herself in Trevor Street, Knightsbridge. My van was almost empty. Just my writing desk, a console table, an antique mirror, a chandelier and two of Emma's guinea pig hutches, were all there was space for in the furnished house I had rented in Lamont Road at Chelsea's World's End. The rest of my share was to go into store.

Emma and Joanna were to live with me at first, as Pat had her new house to arrange. Carol had already settled down in the Wiltshire countryside, and she and a friend farmed a plot of land and kept chickens and goats. Carol was contented with her pastoral life.

Jeremy's world trip had stopped in Israel. The spirit and strange charm of that country had got into him. He had become a religious, Jewish boy. He said Israel was his home.

The problem that remained was to tell Emma and Joanna about Caroline. They had lost their home at a time when they faced the confusion of growing up. I was afraid to unsettle them further by telling them that their father now planned to share his life with someone else.

Caroline disappeared to her father's house in Cornwall, as I had to find a way of telling the girls on my own. So much depended on their reaction to Caroline.

Joanna, who was always straightforward in approach, took the matter in hand. We had only been in Lamont Road for a few days, when she announced: 'We know you've got a girlfriend, dad. Emma and I want to meet her. Won't you bring her round?'

I had underestimated the children. After all those years trying to protect them, it seemed they had known everything all along. Caroline caught the next train back to London.

She arrived in a pair of patchwork trousers, carrying a picnic hamper. It was Emma's thirteenth birthday, and the four of us went off to Chessington Zoo. Caroline adored animals, and I wanted the girls to see her at her best.

She was also good at feeding people. The red-lined hamper bulged with the most mouth-watering food. She had thought of everything, right down to the paper serviettes and patterned plates and cups. Strawberry birthday cakes had been a tradition in our family, and

I must have mentioned it to Caroline, because she had made Emma exactly the right cake.

'She's amazing, dad!'

'Really incredible!'

The girls perched on the arms of the chair into which I sank after taking Caroline back to her flat. After days of worrying about the meeting, I felt in a collapsed state.

Emma and Jo, however, were in high spirits. Caroline was apparently not a bit how they had imagined or, indeed, feared. Not some dreadful, glamorous type, who would have hated having them around.

'Did you see how her hands shook when she drank her tea? She was so nervous, she couldn't eat a thing. And all that marvellous food.'

The fact that Caroline had been more scared of the meeting than the girls had amazed them. They hadn't taken their eyes off her. They hadn't even realized how much my hands had been shaking as well.

I hugged them. It was a precious and very important moment. It meant that nothing now stood between Caroline and me being together for the rest of our lives.

But nothing is ever that simple. Doubts still remained in Caroline's mind. The belief that loving me made up for the loss of everything else had been shaken by my inability to settle down in the Park Lane flat.

Admittedly, I had no home to run back to any more. The family had been divided, but the divorce still hadn't come through, and Caroline couldn't be certain of me until I was no longer a married man.

'Plan your retreat,' John Betjeman once told me. He sat up most of one night, listening to me at the Queen's Hotel in Newton Abbott, after we had done an 'Any Questions' together. The prospect of leaving home again still daunted me, despite the impossibility of remaining with Pat.

'Next time find yourself a house in any area you like,'

John advised. 'Go round there often before you move in. Get to know the place, so you'll look forward to living there.'

The house I had found was a four-bedroomed, Victorian terraced one, just off the King's Road, and further down it than Swanky Jacobs would have liked. I had been spoilt for too long by the tree-lined elegance of Ilchester Place.

Inside, though, it was comfortable enough, with loose-covered sofas and chairs. There wasn't much hard furniture around, but the dining room was cosy, with a round table and deep red walls. Portraits were hung around the place of Viscountess Enfield's family, to whom the house belonged.

Before I moved, I took down the solemn ancestors, with their aquiline noses and expressions of inborn superiority, and replaced them with familiar landscapes from home. My collection of porcelain figures, unearthed in antique shops, I arranged in the drawing room. 'Ambrose', the mascot Caroline and I shared from Skegness, arrived. I had a television set installed. It was an ugly, rented box of laminated wood with a screen that flickered and voices to which I listened without actually taking in a word. But it broke the silence of an empty house. The box was my companion as I sat there on my own, trying to imagine how life would be.

It wasn't a flat. It was a house with a garden, where Shaggy the cairn would run about, and Emma's guinea-pig hutches would be. I moved into Lamont Road, believing it could become a home.

Caroline spent week-ends there with the girls and me, but she wouldn't share my bedroom. She had resented it when her father's second wife, Patricia, had moved into her childhood home to take her mother's place. She didn't want to do anything that might hurt my girls.

Little possessions of hers started appearing round the house. Porcelain dishes, heart-shaped bowls and small jewel cases turned up on my bedroom chest of drawers. A pair of white candlesticks arrived in the dining room. Each time Caroline stayed, she seemed to forget a few more of her clothes.

'Daddy, Charlie's here! She's come for good,' Emma's voice shrieked up the stairs one day. Charlie was also Emma's nickname for Caroline. The child was obsessed with her. She was always slipping round to Caroline's flat. When Caroline stayed at Lamont Road, Emma followed her around the house. Emma had decided Caroline was everything she wanted to be.

I rushed down the stairs to find Caroline in a new coat. The black one had finally disappeared. She had chosen the type I had always imagined she would one day wear. It was a camel-hair coat.

My divorce had just come through, and Caroline had definitely come to stay. She had finally brought her mother's photograph to Lamont Road.

'Dad,' said Jo, 'we know you and Caroline want to be together. You don't need to have separate bedrooms any more.'

We had celebrated my move to Lamont Road by going away on holiday together – a real holiday, certainly the longest in my adult life – for four weeks in Kenya. We stayed with friends in Nairobi, went on a photographic safari and spent two idyllic weeks in what was little better than a straw-roofed hut by the white beaches of Malindi, drove on narrow roads where the only traffic hold-ups were caused by Thompsons gazelles, zebras, giraffes and elephants. One night, driving back from a day fishing on Lake Naivasha, a leopard ran alongside the car, the first time that our host, who had lived in Kenya for twenty-five years, had ever seen one outside a game reserve. Caroline and I felt we really were in luck, and more and more we were becoming a couple.

We flew back to England ready to tackle what lay ahead, together. Emma had found her way to Gatwick Airport to meet us and made it a joyful homecoming.

When we returned Caroline wanted to buy me a dog. I was against it, as I thought we had enough animals already. Apart from Shaggy, there was my grey Persian cat called Smokey Jacobs, and Emma's two guinea-pigs. But Caroline would have filled the house with animals if she had had her way.

And she did have her way, for in the columns of *The Times* there was advertised for sale a litter of golden retriever puppies and Caroline had known that once I had said to Emma, 'You'll know when I'm really happy again when you see me walking alongside my own golden retriever.' We made an appointment with the breeders and off we went to Hertfordshire to see them. They turned out to be a sweet couple with small children living in a mock Georgian Town House who were so in love with their retriever bitch that they wanted just one litter from her and William was one of them. Soon we were to love him as much as was sensibly possible. Shaggy the cairn accepted him immediately and Willy, who was then little more than a ball of soft fur, never noticed in the ensuing months that he became much larger than his highland stepfather, and for the rest of their time together, Shaggy ruled the kennel and Caroline adored them both equally but differently.

She had been right about having him. He brought Lamont Road to life and Caroline and me closer together. He was the first possession we had shared.

Then Christmas 1972 arrived, and I caught pneumonia. Emma was with her mother and Jo had gone to Israel to visit Jeremy. It was to be our first Christmas together, and Caroline had gone wild decorating the house. She became a child again at Christmas. The enormous tree twinkled with tinsel, silver balls and coloured lights.

Holly was everywhere, on top of every picture, arranged in every vase, while bunches of mistletoe hung over doors. The place looked like fairyland.

When my temperature rose to 103°F, Caroline stopped her decorations and started to look after me. She had never seen me look so dreadful. I was so weak, she had to do everything for me, even change my pyjamas and help me sit up in bed, and I felt ashamed.

I was prone to sore throats and stomach disorders, but nothing as serious as this. In my depressed state, I imagined my health had started to deteriorate with age. Caroline shouldn't have been stuck with someone as old as me.

'It doesn't matter what I have to do,' she assured me. 'I want to look after you. You're such a silly, old fruit-cake, I can't help loving you.'

Her touch was so tender. For two days she had never been so gentle. Then Christmas Day arrived and Caroline's mood changed. Christmas meant so much, and it upset her that she hadn't got me well for it.

My temperature had dropped and Caroline insisted that I was better. Admittedly, I tended to panic about my health, but this illness had left me as limp as an old rag. Still, I was determined to alter Caroline's sad face. Feeling the martyr I no doubt looked, I dragged myself downstairs.

Just pulling up my trousers exhausted me. The stairs drained the remainder of my energy. Yet when Caroline found me sagging in a dining-room chair, her expression didn't change.

She had cooked a chicken for lunch. It was all the food there was in the house, as we had been invited for Christmas dinner at friends.

I told her not to expect me to eat anything. The sight of meat sickened me. In my condition, she should have given me a bowl of soup.

'You'll never get better if you don't eat,' she replied

sharply, attacking the chicken with force. She thrust a plate of it in my face. 'And there's no soup.'

I wasn't up to a row. I explained calmly that antibiotics always put me off my food. They made me terribly depressed as well.

Didn't I have a pill to cheer me up? After all, I had enough in the bathroom cabinet to open a chemist's shop.

Caroline's remedy for illness was to curl up in bed and sleep it off. She often accused me of being a hypochondriac, but this just wasn't the moment for me to accept that I was the over-anxious type. All that concerned me was that it would do me no good at all to get worked up.

'You know why I've taken pills,' I said. 'I've needed them in the past two years. I've been through a lot since meeting you.'

'Don't you think I have, too?' Caroline yelled. 'And I'm not stuffed full of bloody pills. The amount you take, I wonder you don't rattle.'

My reaction to any row with Caroline was that I could never marry her. I had been through too many scenes with Pat. Never would I risk that kind of life again, yet there were moments when Caroline and I seemed so far apart.

A tear trickled down her cheek. It almost cured me. I was as disappointed about Christmas as she was. Those blasted decorations were a constant reminder of what it should have been. But being unwell annoyed me as much as it did her.

'I don't exactly enjoy being ill,' I said stiffly.

'You'd be a damn sight better if you stopped thinking about yourself for once,' she replied.

We glared at each other across a table arrangement of mistletoe. As we chewed our chicken in silence, I glanced across at Caroline, and wondered if my face was as long as hers. The thought of it nearly made me laugh. We must have looked such a ludicrous couple, surrounded by all those decorations of hers. But we were so depressed we couldn't even smile.

Caroline came upstairs with a glass of water, when I returned to bed. It was time for the next lot of pills. As I swallowed them, she began to laugh.

'What a bloody awful Christmas,' she cried.

I loved her laugh. All her warmth was in its sound. Of course I wanted to marry her. I still wasn't myself.

Nine

Yet I still didn't buy Caroline an engagement ring. I gave her a lovers' knot instead. It had taken too much to extricate myself from my first marriage, and I couldn't plunge into a second one straight away.

There was still a strangeness about my life which Caroline couldn't help. The wound of losing a home and family still hadn't healed. Depression swept like waves over me, and in those moments I was tormented by everything I had done.

It seemed so unnatural to see Pat's car pull up across the road to drop off the girls. Watching her drive off alone brought back the guilt. I had taken so much from my wife as well.

I was a man of habit and the habits of a lifetime had gone. Some mornings I woke and in those first, confused moments of coming out of sleep, thought I was back in Ilchester Place with my family in the kitchen downstairs. There were so many memories, it was hard to begin again.

Some old friends avoided me. They were ones whose own marriages were in trouble. What I had done seemed too close to home. There was an awkwardness about seeing anyone Pat and I had known. It was difficult to be natural with Caroline, make any gestures of affection towards her, when they had known me as a family man.

Caroline, too, felt the strain. She was being judged as the girl who had taken me from Pat.

Divorce is costly, and I wasn't earning the large sums I once had. By the time I finished paying for all my new commitments, there wasn't much left. I ran two homes; Emma had gone to boarding school, and I paid the fees; and I supported my parents as well.

My earnings had dropped drastically when I needed more money than at any time in my life, but it wasn't just the lost income that worried me about the decline in my career. I had not one show on television, and even personal appearances had dropped off as I wasn't the regular on television I had once been. There were still my radio programmes, and in between I kept myself busy with charity shows, which earned me nothing at all.

A job like mine is inevitably insecure. Even in the sixties, at the peak of my career, there was always the worry of how long it would last. When the work stopped coming in, it seemed proof of all my fears. My face had gone out of fashion; I would never be able to work my way back. There was already such a sense of failure about my life that I saw every contract as my last.

When I told Michael Bowen, the producer of 'Any Questions', about the coming divorce, I said I would understand if he thought I should leave the show. He found my reaction absurd; no one ever bothered about things like that any more.

For years I had worried about what people might think about my private life. So much vanity accompanies fame that I thought everyone cared about what I was really like. Yet when the story of the divorce appeared in the newspapers, only a handful of unpleasant letters arrived. They were cranky ones, telling me to go back to my wife. But we were still so vulnerable, they upset us all the same.

The only person to blame for the state of my career

was me. Being torn between Caroline and my family for so long, I just hadn't put the effort into my job. In all ways, I had to build a life again.

Caroline and I did settle at Lamont Road. My life-style had inevitably changed. I wasn't surrounded by servants any more, but there was a cosiness about Caroline returning from work with loaded shopping baskets to cook our evening meal.

She had a job with Theo Cowan, the theatrical press agent, at that time, and dealt with some of his well-known clients. She was too honest for the artificial compliments and egos that need constant flattery. She preferred what was genuine and real.

Our suppers, which were always massive ones, were brought up on trays to the drawing room, so we could watch television while we ate. Caroline had become an addict. We had a portable set in the bedroom, which she watched while I slept. It was a convenient arrangement, as I didn't have to worry about having to keep awake.

Some evenings we strolled arm in arm around the neighbourhood, window-shopping in the Fulham Road, watching youngsters parading in their weird clothes, the studs in flashy cars talent-spotting amongst the dolly girls. Usually, we ended up at the Pizza House on the corner.

We became quite attached to that little corner of London life. We got used to the noise of buses tusning into our street, and the 'gay' lavatory nearby. The shopkeepers started treating us as regulars.

We made new friends, mostly younger ones than I had had before. They fell between the twenty-one years that separated Caroline's age from mine. Dick Marsh and his Caroline were regular callers, and there were often dinner parties in the red-walled dining room at

Lamont Road, when laughter warmed the house. A house becomes a home when friends start dropping in, and Caroline and I weren't isolated any more; we were becoming an accepted couple.

Unfortunately, it wasn't possible to remain at Lamont Road. The house was on a year's lease. I had put a deposit on a house which was being built on a small estate in Putney, which was moderately priced, but it was an ugly, characterless place, and neither of us liked it.

We went to look over a house at Launceston Place in Kensington, which happened to be just round the corner from Caroline's old flat. It was in one of those smart, tree-lined roads again. The house itself was Georgian, white-fronted, with slim bay windows and white stone steps leading up to the front door. By Ilchester Place standards, it wasn't large: there were four bedrooms, a basement kitchen and dining room, and a drawing room which stretched across the length of the house. But it had the charm and elegance of its age.

It was also wildly uneconomical. The house was on a short lease, which would take most of the capital I had left. The owner, however, was clever: she realized at once how much we liked the house. She said she was going out that evening. Why didn't we come over and spend a few hours there alone. That way we would know if we really wanted the house.

She left some pâté and a bottle of red wine. It was a warm, May evening, and the small, courtyard garden was heavy with the scent of white blossom and early summer flowers.

We fell in love with the house that evening, and more in love with each other. Caroline was persuasive when she got me in a romantic mood. She rushed back to Lamont Road to start making plans.

That we couldn't really afford the house didn't worry her. Caroline had worked in television, and she was wise about my career. She understood its unpredictability, and while fame didn't impress her, she respected the way I did my job. She was convinced that once I was myself again, the contracts would start rolling in.

What she was less certain about, however, was when I was going to marry her. I didn't mention the subject, and neither did she, but the thought of it was always there, like an unspoken barrier between us. I still didn't feel ready and, sensing that, Caroline started to become unsure of herself again.

The girls had become a problem between us. Emma and Joanna were often as difficult as teenage girls can be, since the initial novelty of Caroline and a new house had worn thin and home life had become as ordinary and everyday as it had always been.

Jo had left school, not knowing what job she wanted, and she spent all her time mooning and making a mess around the house, which infuriated us. When Emma was home from boarding school, the two girls constantly fought. Emma had adopted a worldly, superior air which maddened Jo. Even as the older of the two, Jo was far too straightforward and vulnerable to out-manoeuvre the subtlety of Emma.

Emma, always a picture of neatness herself, tormented Jo about her scruffy looks. Unable to get her own back with words, Jo's method became physical attack, and often I had to prise the two of them apart. Even then, Emma always had the last word: she knew how to hurt Joanna most.

Caroline hadn't taken into account being landed with a ready-made family, and a difficult one at that. It was hardly surprising at times she couldn't cope, when often Emma and Jo were beyond me as well. But Caroline took it personally: she blamed her lack of authority with the girls on not being my wife.

Often, at tender moments, I had longed to give Caroline my child, but seldom any more. Emma and Jo were enough trouble. At my age, it seemed impossible to start another family when I couldn't even cope with the one I had got.

At their ages, Caroline had still been a child, a strictly brought-up, well-behaved girl with a pony-tail and long socks. The rules from her childhood, such as only using the drawing room at certain times and being in bed before ten, just couldn't work with Emma and Jo.

To Caroline, it was totally unfair. What she needed was not my daughters, but children of her own. But if I married her, the girls came too.

I returned one Friday evening, longing for the peace of home. That particular 'Any Questions' programme had been a difficult one, as two of the panel hadn't got on. They had tried to take out their dislike of each other on the air, and it had been hard keeping control. On top of that, I had the irritation of a slow train, which stopped at every station on the way home.

A nightcap was what I needed, and then straight to bed. Emma was waiting in the drawing room for me. She should have been at boarding school.

'Daddy,' she cried, flinging her arms around me, 'I can't bear school. I want to live here with Charlie and you.'

Emma was behaving badly at school. She wouldn't work. She disobeyed rules. She slipped home without permission whenever she could. The headmistress had already written, threatening to ask her to be taken away from the school.

'I was only sent to boarding school to get me out of the way,' Emma continued in her plaintive voice. She always reminded me of a portrait of a Victorian child with ringlets and an exquisite face, which hung in the drawing room at home when Emma was born. But for all her innocence, Emma already had a woman's guile. She almost made me forget that she was the one who had pleaded to go to boarding school. Though I have to admit that it had been convenient to have her out of the way at the time.

My reaction to both Emma's and Jo's naughtiness was still tinged by guilt. Growing up was difficult enough without having to lose their home as well. Also, if I was too angry with Emma, she went straight round to Pat. She was clever at using the two of us against each other.

I told her off for coming home from school, but I added that I realized that she was unhappy there. I liked being given time to think a problem through. I promised that I would look into finding a school near home.

'Daddy, you're lovely.' When she got what she wanted, Emma had such charm.

'Where's Charlie?'

'Washing up.'

The sound of plates and cups crashing in the kitchen sink warned me that Caroline was in a mood. The kitchen was Caroline's domain. She hated being helped in there, but like most women she still moaned because no one offered a hand.

Had I seen the state Jo had made of the drawing room? All I wanted was bed, so I tried to change the subject and avoid a scene. I told her that I was thinking about taking Emma away from boarding school. I didn't expect that to anger Caroline, as she and Emma still got on well.

'And then I'll spend the rest of my life clearing up after the two of them. I'm no more than a bloody housekeeper here. I've tried so hard to make a nice home, but it's impossible with those two around.'

Tidy though I was, Caroline was fanatical.

What she had to accept was that this was the girls'

home now, as well as hers. She couldn't expect Emma and Jo to do everything she said.

You always put your daughters first. You always take their side!' she cried.

Schools were a favourite topic with her, and she reverted to it as she finished the washing-up. Caroline was certain Jo's comprehensive school was to blame for her lack of discipline and direction in life. All schools like that taught children was about sex and drugs. Jo's opinion that most girls of fourteen should be on the pill had shocked Caroline. Caroline hadn't even known what the word meant at that age. She felt that if I took Emma away from a decent school, she would become exactly the same.

Caroline and I differed over so many things. The right school mattered to her. It had really upset her when her father couldn't quite afford to send her to Wycombe Abbey, an exclusive girls' school, where most of her friends had gone.

She stuck to all the principles she had been brought up to respect. She never changed an opinion, and neither did I.

'What's important to me is not the type of school, but whether my children are happy there,' I said.

'Do what you want! You always do! I never have any say in this house. I often wonder what the hell I'm doing here.'

She stared hard at me, waiting for some reassurance about her place in my life. But all I wanted was some peace. To end this particular argument with Caroline, a gesture had to come from me. I shouted upstairs to Jo. A henna-ed head of ringlets appeared over the stairs. A pair of wide, grey eyes regarded me. For all her hippy looks, Jo still had the loveliest face. It wasn't easy to be hard on my girls.

'Go and tidy your mess in the drawing room,' I said,

in as stern a voice as I could muster. 'You know how it upsets us when you leave things lying around.'

'Dad,' Jo replied wearily, 'I spend my life here straightening cushions. I only have to drink a cup of coffee and Caroline expects me to leap up and wash the cup.'

I pointed at the drawing room. 'I'm too tired for any more rows,' I replied.

I went upstairs to bed. Just as I had started to drop off the front door slammed with a violence that shook the bed. Jo had taken her temper out into the night.

Caroline came up to bed much later. She lay stiffly beside me, for though her pride wouldn't allow her to admit it, she hated upsetting Jo. Jo had so many of Caroline's qualities. She was honest and vulnerable, too. Caroline often spent hours talking to her about the problems of growing up.

With Jo's weird taste in clothes, it was hard to buy her anything she'd ever wear, but Caroline had the patience to search out the kind of T-shirts and clogs Jo liked. She had even helped to teach her to cook.

Caroline cared for both the girls and what they grew up to be. She tried to teach them to stick by what they believed in. To Caroline, other people's opinions weren't important, so long as she did what she believed was right.

It wasn't the girls who had let Caroline down. It was me.

It seemed madness to move to a new house with those three. All it meant was transferring the rows to another house. We did, however, move to Launceston Place. It happened during a rare moment of peace in our lives, when Emma had returned to boarding school and Jo disappeared into the country to stay with friends. Without the girls around, Caroline and I always got on better, as there wasn't so much to argue about.

I had excited Caroline with descriptions of all the elegant furniture I had in store. When the shabby collection of odds and ends arrived at Launceston Place, I hardly believed it was mine.

'That's not my chair!' I exclaimed, as an ugly, ragged-covered object was carted in. Caroline's face began to drop. All I recognized about what I had thought was a brand-new cooker was its clock. Everything had looked different at Ilchester Place, and I had picked all the worst stuff in my haste to leave that house.

The removal men left. Rows of dusty packing cases stood against the freshly painted walls. We perched on top of one and surveyed the drawing room, imagining what it could become.

I took Caroline's hand. 'It'll be a lovely house,' I said.

'A real home,' she replied.

Everything would be different now.

Ten

On Monday, 23 February 1973, Caroline and I spent a quiet evening at Launceston Place. I watched television while she sewed name tabs into some new school vests for Emma.

It was eight months since the move. The old chairs had fresh white and green covers which matched the curtains. The walls were terracotta-coloured, and there was the same green sofa on which Caroline had sat that first evening I had taken her to Ilchester Place. 'Ambrose' stood amongst the porcelain. The drawing room looked like a summer house, it was so full of plants and flowers.

The girls were away again. Emma was still at boarding school, and Joanna was staying at her mother's. As much as I loved them, how I relished those quiet times.

Caroline finished her needlework, and went up early to bed. We both reached for our books on the bedside table and read for a while. The photograph of Caroline's mother stared down at us from the chest of drawers. We seemed such an established couple sitting side by side in our own bed. It seemed ridiculous I still hadn't got round to marrying her.

Caroline's arms held me while I fell asleep. I didn't need sleeping tablets any longer or, indeed, pills of any kind. I had become my old self again.

The telephone's ring came from far away. I had been

in those first, deep moments of sleep, and my hand fumbled around the bedside table. I found the receiver and picked it up.

A loud voice spoke: 'Is that you, David?'

'Yes,' I murmured. What could anyone want at that time of night?

'It's Jack here. Jack Hirschkopf.'

It was an American voice. The name was familiar. Then I remembered. It was Jeremy's new father-in-law. My son had recently married an American girl called Shelley in Israel.

'Hi, Jack,' I replied.

Caroline switched on the bedside light. It was past one o'clock. Jack was phoning from New York. He couldn't have realized the time in Launceston Place.

'It's Jeremy,' he said. 'I've got some terrible news.'

'What's the boy been up to?' I asked.

Caroline was putting on a blue linen dressing gown with white *broderie anglaise* around the edge.

'He's gone.' Jack's voice sounded terrible.

'Where's he gone?' I asked. I couldn't understand Jeremy leaving Israel. He wouldn't have left the place where he felt that he belonged.

'Oh, God,' Jack groaned. 'I don't mean that. He's dead. Killed. Run over by a car.'

'I'll ring you back,' I said. I replaced the receiver.

I must have told Caroline. I remember the horror in her face. She didn't seem to cry. She stared helplessly at me, not knowing what to do.

I rushed out of the bedroom and down the stairs. Then I ran up the stairs. I ran up and down them, shouting and screaming for my son.

Caroline stood in the bedroom doorway, tears pouring down her face. Her expression urged me to keep running. Silently she told me to run up and down those stairs.

Finally, she held me. I wanted to stay in her arms, but I couldn't. I had to get Jack on the phone again. It might have been a mistake.

An Israeli army car killed Jeremy. It came round the bend of a narrow road in the village of Migdal, where Jeremy lived. His house was at the top of the hill. It was evening. He had been walking home, tired after a day's work.

He had tried to jump out of the way when he heard the car's approach. Cars are driven on a different side of the road in Israel. Jeremy was an English boy. Instinct made him jump the wrong way.

The driver was a boy of nineteen. He was the same age as my son.

Once Jeremy wrote that he was going to die. It was at his first boarding school.

Dear Mummy and Daddy. My heart is breaking. Last night I cried so much, my tears soaked my pillow. I shall probably die of pneumonia.

I had to tell his mother.

Caroline got out my clothes. As she helped me into my overcoat, I asked, 'You won't worry, will you?'

She was so precious to me. I couldn't survive this without her.

I rang the doorbell at Trevor Street. It echoed like a wail through the dark house. A bedroom light went on. Another blazed in the hall.

Pat opened the front door. I hadn't seen her for months. She was wearing a blue jersey dressing gown, and she looked thin and drawn.

My face told her. 'Which one?' she asked.

'Jeremy.'

I expected her to faint, but instead her body froze. She didn't move, but there was the sound of sobbing. She went into my arms. Her body was hard and brittle, but gradually the tears came.

Joanna was asleep upstairs. I roused her. I told Carol on the phone. Emma slept at boarding school. She was still so young, the shock would have been too much by telephone.

I made more calls. Pat's brother arrived. A car set off for Fovant to fetch Carol. Pat and I were booked on the morning flight to Tel Aviv.

All the time I worried about Caroline. She would be wondering what was happening. I didn't want her to be alone.

The furniture of my marriage was around Pat's house. It was just someone else's furniture. I was a stranger there. There was no comfort from Pat and I having shared a son. We were even further apart now Jeremy had gone.

I was desperate to get back to Caroline. I wanted to go home. No taxis were about, so I hurried through Knightsbridge. The wide, deserted street was bathed in the fluorescent orange of tall street-lights. Shapes of dummies stood like ghosts in darkened shop windows, their glassy eyes following me as I passed.

A boy in cricket whites was one of them. His immovable, plastic hands gripped the handle of a cricket bat. Jeremy had once looked like that. His face glowed when he walked on to the school cricket pitch.

It was the fathers' day match. He had been the first to bat. I bowled the first ball. He hit it straight back. Instinct made me catch it: I hadn't meant to shatter his pride.

Caroline was waiting at home. She was so tender. I remembered the hardness of Pat's body that night. If only she had someone to hold her as I had.

My arms tightened around Caroline. The thought of losing her terrified me. She might think Jeremy's death would make me closer to Pat.

'You won't worry about Pat and I being together in Israel?' I asked.

She looked gently at me. 'You must go to your son,' she said. 'And you must go with his mother.'

Next morning, Caroline left to fetch Emma from

school. Despite the rows at home, Emma still cared so much for her, and Caroline was the one to tell her that her brother was dead.

Caroline was also looking after Carol and Joanna. All my girls would be together. I was leaving them behind.

On the plane, I tried to hold Pat's hand, but I couldn't get any feeling from it. I began to weep.

'Pull yourself together,' Pat said. 'Stop making an exhibition of yourself.'

We never stopped attacking each other. Our fights had driven Jeremy away. He hadn't even wanted to meet Caroline. He had been through too much. He didn't want to be involved with our problems any more.

He had met her once and I'm not sure that he realized it – we were walking together in Richmond Park and I had prearranged with Caroline and Tanya that we should meet accidentally on purpose – they did little more than shake hands, and say hello but at least their paths had crossed and they had touched each other.

I remembered how he had sat up all night before he left on his world trip, sewing himself a canvas bag. He packed it with a couple of pairs of jeans, a few T-shirts and not much else. Possessions never bothered him.

Next morning, Joanna had gone down to the Tube station to see him off.

'Wherever you are,' I told him, 'there will always be a return ticket waiting for you to come home.'

He hadn't travelled far. He had found refuge in a country which lived in constant threat of extinction, bruised and battered by past wars. In Israel, Jeremy had found someone in whom he could believe. He had discovered God.

His letters home became religious tracts. He even wanted to be a rabbi. An Israeli friend of his visited Caroline and me when he was in London. He spoke of Jeremy as a holy boy.

His room in Jerusalem had become a meeting place for drug addicts, the homeless, anyone in trouble. He worked long hours at a home for the mentally disturbed.

I had found it hard to understand. 'He never had time for religion before,' I told Caroline. 'He was so good at cricket and sports. He was a normal English boy.'

'It sounds as if he's suffering from a religious mania,' Caroline replied. 'He's going to need you when he comes out of it.'

Tzafrir Anbar, a colonel in the Israeli Army, waited at Tel Aviv airport with the British Consul and his wife. They hurried Pat and me through Customs and into a car which was to take us on the four-hour journey to Jeremy's village, where his wife Shelley waited.

There was a child as well. Jeremy's son was six months old. He was called Azriel, which in Hebrew means 'with the help of God'. I had never seen my grandson.

Tzafrir's shoulders in his khaki army uniform jutted above the driver's seat. He had become a friend on my first visit to Israel after the Six Days War. He was tall and lean, with a clean-cut face that reminded me of John Newcombe, the tennis player, except that Tzafrir had managed to grow a ginger moustache.

He was a kindly man. He had even been concerned about wearing his army uniform in front of me, as it had been a soldier who killed my son.

The bodies of dogs lay beside the road, killed by passing cars, just as Jeremy had been. But no one cared about them. Their bodies rotted under the constant sun.

We passed olive groves, and rocky, red-soiled countryside with grass dried stiff in the mid-day heat. Cypress trees marked cemeteries, like stately guardians of the dead.

I had driven through countryside like that the last time I had visited Jeremy. He begged me to see the place where he worked. It was a community called the Swedish Village, which lay just outside Jerusalem.

Jeremy had waited for me at the gates. He was a tall boy, who had grown pathetically thin. He had become a vegan. He wouldn't eat nourishing meat, milk and eggs. He fed his dog in the same way, poor emaciated thing.

Jeremy's tiny face, hidden by a long shock of dark hair, was still a gentle, boyish one. But his eyes, which had always been intense, now gleamed with a strange light.

Lines of white-walled huts, shaded by olive trees, stood in the compound of the Swedish Village, which was surrounded by a high fence. People jumped out from behind the trees as we walked past. Some had ugly, distorted bodies and childlike faces. There were giants of men with the expression of sad clowns. They hugged Jeremy. They picked him up. They slobbered over him. Their expressions of love terrified me.

A nurse called Jeremy. A man screamed uncontrollably in one of the huts. He was a fleshless being with burning eyes. Jeremy didn't speak. He held the bony body in his arms and calmed him by the tranquillity in his face. Those people with their sick minds were the ones Jeremy had found to love.

The journey to Migdal was almost over. In the distance stretched green, rolling hills. The sea of Lake Tiberius shimmered under a blue sky.

Jeremy's village was near Tiberius. He had gone there to study clinical child psychology. He had given up the idea of being a rabbi when he became a married man.

Shelley was inside the house with her parents, who had arrived before us from New York. Jeremy's home was a small, whitewashed place with two rooms and a scullery, not much bigger than a hut. My grandson slept in a corner, in a white-sided cot.

The baby was breathing badly. He had a snuffly cold. Jeremy had written so much about the miracle of birth.

This was the child he had left behind. But there was no one who could replace my son.

Shelley was hysterical with grief. She was a handsome, powerful girl. Jack Hirschkopf was chairman of a group of companies in the States; his daughter was used to having everything. I hadn't really wanted her to have Jeremy.

When she became pregnant, the wedding was a rushed affair. Pat, Joanna and Carol went. I stayed at home with Caroline and Emma. My excuse was that I couldn't just pack my bag and dash to Israel, but it had been more than not having the time.

Shelley loved Jeremy, but she was young: there would be someone else for her. I had known Jeremy all his life. I didn't want any other son.

There was sunlight outside, and too much emotion in that house. I walked up a hill and sat down on the dried grass. Jeremy had dug a vegetable patch behind his house. Little green shoots burst through the richly coloured earth.

Caroline, too, was always in the garden at home, sometimes even after dark, planting shrubs and seeds. Like Jeremy, she loved all living things. He wouldn't be around to see his vegetables grow.

A shaded path ran behind the house. Fig trees cut out the sun. It felt quite dark and chill. A minibus was parked there. It was a shabby vehicle, smeared with mud and dust. As I walked past, I glanced inside.

Jeremy lay on the floor of the minibus, his body wrapped in a white shroud. His face was covered, but every line of his body told me it was him.

I started to scream. I kicked the side of the bus. 'It's pagan. Heathen,' I cried.

Tzafrir was behind me. He never let me out of his sight.

'Didn't you know this was our custom?' he said. 'Except for soldiers, we don't use coffins here.'

I couldn't take my eyes off Jeremy. How thin he was. He had given me so much happiness. Now there was only unbearable pain.

Caroline wanted a child of mine so much. But I could never bring anyone else into the world who could make me so vulnerable again.

There was a commotion outside Jeremy's house. Two coaches had arrived from Jerusalem, bringing people who had known Jeremy there. The whole village had turned out as well. At least two hundred people waited outside the house.

There were students in T-shirts and jeans, men in dark suits, some in open-necked shirts and casual trousers. The women were dressed in simple cotton frocks and skirts.

These people all knew about death. Every family in Israel has been touched by it. Each one understood what it meant to have someone killed simply because he was an Israeli and a Jew. The Israeli way is to be unafraid of death. To confront it and exorcise it, just as I was about to be forced to do.

Jeremy was lifted down from the minibus. I grabbed a handle of the stretcher. The crowd started to wail and howl. People bore down on me, trying to snatch the stretcher. I didn't know it was an honour to carry it, but nothing on earth would have made me let it go.

In a mass, we started down the hill for the cemetery. There were two miles to walk. People pushed and jostled to get near Jeremy. Some still tried to wrest the stretcher from my hands.

Pat and Shelley walked behind. Three times we stopped to pray. The words had been written phonetically for me, but I couldn't say them. I kept breaking down.

Some faces close to me I recognized. They were the same people who had called to Jeremy, when we walked together through the old quarter of Jerusalem. They had touched his face. They had kissed me for being the father of a holy boy.

Jeremy and I had gone to the Wailing Wall together. Jeremy rubbed his face in the stone, chanting softly. I took him in my arms. I was sobbing, not in sadness, but in real joy. Because it meant so much to him, I had felt the meaning of that sacred place. 'Some months ago,' I told him, 'my father died in my arms. I have come to life in yours.'

Now his feet were close to me. The stretcher was like lead. The pain in my arm was unbearable, but I wouldn't let go.

Suddenly, though I still held the stretcher, I couldn't feel its weight. It was almost as if God had felt my pain. I must have walked ten paces before I realized what had happened. Once again, Tzafrir helped me. He was walking sideways down the hill, holding the stretcher up.

We passed through the gates of the small cemetery, ringed by those soft, green hills. Jeremy's freshly dug grave waited. We lowered his body into it.

People began to whisper. Finally a man hurried off.

'He's gone to fetch Jeremy's shoes,' Tzafrir told me. 'He can't be buried without them.'

I couldn't stand there, looking down at that thin, young body, so unprotected and alone in the earth. How much more did these people expect me to suffer? These were their customs, not mine.

'Take my shoes,' I said. 'Bury him with mine.'

'They must be his,' Tzafrir replied, 'for on them is his blood.'

Jeremy's plimsolls were old and dirty. They looked pathetic beside him in the grave. Then I was handed a spade. I was beyond tears. Inwardly I sobbed, but I didn't make a sound. The weight of grief was too great to cry aloud.

Then someone with a razor slit my shirt. It was a

hand-made shirt with my initials on it. I stared uncomprehendingly at Tzafrir.

'Rend your shirt,' he whispered.

I wanted to tear it. I ripped and ripped until only little pieces remained on the ground. Tears poured down my face.

Then it was over, and I stood quietly by the grave. The pain had been released, and I felt the warmth of the sun again. I began to understand what this terrible piece of theatre had been about.

There is too much pain in Israel to be kept inside. To survive, the people force the suffering out. Pain remains, but in a muted way. It is what Israelis bear all their lives.

I walked across to Pat and Shelley. Pat stood like a statue, staring at the grave.

Caroline had phoned Tzafrir's house several times to find out how I was. Two days later, I flew home. Pat was going with Shelley and her parents to a resort in Israel. Pat and Shelley got on well. I was the outsider with both of them.

All the girls waited for me at Heathrow Airport. As we drove back home, I said, 'One thing's certain. Jeremy must be a saint in heaven now.'

'And Caroline's a saint on earth,' Joanna replied.

Caroline hadn't known Jeremy, but she had wept for him as well. She had taken each one of the girls to her bed at night to comfort them. She talked to them about how close her mother still felt to her. Now Jeremy would watch over the girls.

Unbeknown to Pat, Caroline had furnished a nursery at Pat's home for my grandson when he came to London with Shelley.

Caroline had given so much to me and my children. Yet I had returned from Israel convinced that I could never marry her.

I could not deny her the children she wanted, but I

was convinced that I could never have another child. Jeremy had been so special. Like Caroline, he had the gift of extra loving. It would be impossible to replace him with another son.

'You mustn't worry about Jeremy,' Caroline told me. 'Loving God so much, he must have gone straight to Him.'

Eleven

Caroline and I were having dinner in the country with friends called Gerry and Janie Thomas, and Caroline was getting merry. She always spoke slowly when on the odd occasion she'd had a few too many, pronouncing each word with care, but the real give-away was her head: she had a long neck, and in a slightly tipsy state it wasn't easy to balance her head on top of it. The more she drank, the more her head began to nod.

Gerry offered another brandy, but it was time for us to leave. It was all right for Caroline, being able to lie in bed all next morning, but I had to be in town for my early morning Sunday radio programme, 'Melodies for You'.

Caroline hated me making decisions for the two of us in front of other people. She accused me of treating her like a child. 'I'd love another brandy,' she said. I sat down again.

She had ignored me all evening. She was always testing me lately, pushing me towards the limit of what I could stand, so one day I really would turn round and tell her to get out of my life.

In the six months since Jeremy's death she had become convinced I would never marry her. I explained that she had to give me time to recover, but Caroline's patience had been stretched too far. She no longer believed that time would change anything between us.

There were no plans to talk about. The future stretched as far as whether we would still be together tomorrow, and so all we did was quarrel. An emptiness had crept into our lives, which I knew only too well.

But I wasn't going to oblige her with a row in front of friends. I continued talking to Gerry, while keeping an eye on the level of Caroline's glass. She took maddeningly small sips.

Her mood had altered directly we had arrived. The Thomases' small son, Max, was in pyjamas, waiting up for us. I took him in my arms. I couldn't help making a fuss of him. He reminded me of Jeremy at the same age. It upset and angered Caroline to see my affection for someone else's child when it could have been our own.

Caroline finished the brandy. Then she lit a cigarette. She had smoked far too much already. If she didn't leave at once, I'd walk out, and that would be that.

I stood up again. My expression must have warned Caroline it was time to go and, with a sulky face, she started collecting her things.

'What the hell am I doing with a man as old as you?' she rounded on me, as soon as we were inside the car.

She made that remark so often lately that I had begun to feel guilty about being middle-aged. There was a time when she had made me feel young again, but now she constantly harped on how she missed her young friends.

I was always the first to leave a party. I never took her dancing because it meant staying up too late. I knew I had changed, but she made me sound a terrible bore.

Money had become another sore point with us. She was sick of hearing about what I had once earned, the wonderful houses I had owned, the lavishness of my former social life. But for my blasted family, as she then referred to them, we wouldn't be so bloody hard up. I was so eaten up with guilt, I was paying them off with almost every penny I earned.

'My life consists of waiting on you and your daughters. When did you ever buy me anything? I notice, though, that darling Emma never has to ask twice for a new dress.'

Since Emma had left boarding school and lived at home, she could do nothing right as far as Caroline was concerned. Admittedly Emma felt the same. From thinking Caroline was perfection, Emma now saw her at the other extreme. Emma was older, too. They both wanted their own way.

'I know I'm a mean sod, and I spend nothing on you,' I burst out. 'Well, that's nearly the truth, except that we've shared just about everything else.'

It was living with Caroline I paid for, and quite expensive living at that. I couldn't compete with her rich friends, because I hadn't their money, and they hadn't the commitments I had got. But we had a nice home. We went out to expensive places. We had holidays abroad. When it came down to it, I doubted if those friends of hers lived much differently from us.

Now she had got me started, there were a lot of home truths to tell Caroline. I was sick of always being put on the defensive. Each time we argued, it was as if she pushed me up against a wall. What amazed me was that she attacked the principles which she respected herself. If she hadn't, we wouldn't have lasted more than a few nights together.

My marriage was the only contract I had ever broken, and I didn't need constant reminding of that. But it wasn't guilt that made me support my family, it was a need to do what I believed was right. I couldn't have lived with myself otherwise.

I tried to explain this sense of responsibility in a way that she could feel it herself. Say we were married, I told her, and we had a child. Then for some reason we were parted. Her death would serve as an example of that. Then I would care for our child in the same way as I looked after the children I already had.

It might happen later that I decided to share my life with someone else, but it would make no difference to my caring for our child. That woman would have to know that that was my way, even though it might be hell for her, just as it was for Caroline coping with my daughters now.

Caroline stared in front of her. In the darkness of the car, the outline of her face had grown sad. Finally she spoke: 'But we will never have a child,' she replied.

The car was outside Launceston Place. I didn't have to reply, and there was no answer I could give that she didn't already know.

Directly we got indoors, Caroline walked into the drawing room. 'No records tonight,' I pleaded.

A habit of hers lately was to stay up all night playing romantic tunes to herself. She smoked and drank and danced alone in the drawing room, while I lay under the bedcovers upstairs, furiously trying to shut out the noise.

'I feel like dancing,' she replied. Her moods swung like a pendulum. By the time I reached the bedroom, the floorboards vibrated with sound.

This was Caroline's way of taking out all her resentment. I hadn't behaved fairly. If I couldn't bring myself to marry her, then I should have set her free. But emotions don't take fairness into account.

I couldn't imagine life without her. Our love was still there, buried under all those rows. But the way she behaved, the last thing I could risk was marrying her. She couldn't force me into a decision I was still unable to make.

I'd taken enough from her that evening. The incessant beat of music thundered like a war drum inside my head. I leapt out of bed and down the stairs.

'How can anyone be so bloody selfish?' I exploded. Caroline had reduced me to swearing as well.

Her back confronted me. It swayed in time to some soppy, romantic tune. She turned slowly, her body still moving to the rhythm. Tears streamed down her face.

Immediately, I wanted her. 'Darling,' I cried. 'What am I doing to you?'

She came to bed with me. We made love through her tears. I was taking her youth. I wasn't the man she'd expected me to be.

On reflection it is obvious to me now that our troubles were often caused by me. It isn't easy to wear a public face and be on parade unless at times you can let off steam, and the place for that is at home. And my moods set the atmosphere in the house. When I was cheerful, Caroline became more like her old self. Even the girls weren't as difficult. But when the failure of my life caught up with me, the place resounded with the rows.

Caroline and I started to get on better as my career picked up. From having no shows on television, I suddenly found myself with three. They were called 'Where Are They Now?', 'Who, What or Where' and 'What's My Line?' There must have been something lucky in the letter 'w' for me.

I was also in demand by ladies' luncheon clubs, and so many were there, it could be a lifetime's work giving talks to each one of them. Being of a certain age had widened my appeal. I had weathered the slump in my career, and was becoming an established broadcaster, not just the man who had once scored the 'hits' and 'misses' on the 'Juke Box Jury' show.

Being busy always makes me feel secure, and I enjoyed the sight of contracts rolling in. I started travelling a lot again, and I returned home to Caroline's warmth.

I started writing her little notes again. Had I told her in the last five minutes that I loved her? Romance was a necessary part of life for both Caroline and me. I left the notes around the house for her to find, and she kept each one in a bedroom drawer. We were in love again.

Shortly after Christmas 1973, Peter and Mary Noble came for Sunday lunch. The Christmas tree was still decorated and our spirits high. Thinking back, Emma and Jo were also away.

Caroline sparkled. She always was at her best making people happy, and she cooked the most elaborate meal.

The Nobles left, and I went upstairs to sleep off the effects of too much food and wine while Caroline did the clearing up. But I couldn't sleep, thinking about her. Lately there had been so much laughter in the house.

She loved thinking up surprises, just to see the pleasure on my face. There was my birthday party. I guessed something was going on when I spotted Caroline whispering with the girls. Then I opened the cupboard where she had hidden my strawberry birthday cake and ruined the whole thing.

She ordered me a blazer. It was a blue one with a paisley lining, and the tailor, who had made my clothes for twenty years, managed it without a single fitting. The only mistake was the buttons. They were Army ones, and I had served in the Navy.

Those buttons ruined the blazer for Caroline. She was absurdly upset. She was such a perfectionist herself, she expected everyone else to be the same.

'We'll be the perfect couple,' I remembered her telling me. Neither of us could get around to marriage until everything was exactly right.

Yet what would I have done without her in the last four years? She could be endlessly patient with me. She'd listened for hours while I talked about Jeremy. I probably repeated the same things over and over again, but just talking about him had taken away so much pain. She always assured me he was still close to me, and in those quiet moments together, I believed it, too.

She and Jeremy were so alike. They were the givers

in the world. He would have liked her; he would have wanted her to have my child.

Emma was still a problem, as she and Caroline still didn't get along, but Emma was almost grown up. I couldn't keep putting my children first. Now it was Caroline's turn. I was absurd not to have married her. Much younger men than I would have jumped at the chance.

I got out of bed, still warmed by the lunchtime wine. It had been a perfect day so far, and I wanted it to end that way.

Caroline was in the kitchen, her hands plunged in the washing-up bowl. She wore a long, striped apron over a brown dress and her hair was tied back.

I addressed the back of her head. 'I've got something to ask,' I said. 'It's a question that's long overdue.' I paused and asked quietly, 'Will you marry me?'

Caroline's hands remained in the washing-up. Tears began to plop into the water.

She turned, laughing and crying, and flung her arms round me. Her hands were soaking wet. 'I thought you'd never ask!' she cried.

The phone rang. It was Peter, thanking us for lunch. 'We're engaged,' Caroline shouted down the phone. I couldn't believe it myself.

An engagement party was hurriedly arranged for the same night. We celebrated at the White Elephant on the river. Next morning we were the first to arrive at Kensington Registry Office to book the date. It was to be Wednesday of the following week. Having waited so long, now every day unmarried seemed like a waste.

I expected an old-fashioned girl like Caroline to want an antique engagement ring. Instead, she chose a modern diamond one. She could have had a bigger diamond: the way I felt, I would have bought her any ring in the shop. But it seemed as if she had picked that particular ring long before. She had been planning her wedding day ever since she was a child.

Caroline wanted our names and dates inscribed inside the plain gold wedding ring, but the jeweller in the Burlington Arcade advised us to wait until after the event. After all, something might happen to change the date.

'Perhaps you're right,' I said.

Caroline's wedding dress was pure Caroline. It was a Jaeger dress in cream wool and very understated. The red fox-fur hat was more surprising, and she had a matching borrowed muff. She had been so disappointed about not being able to afford the two that the shop had lent the muff for her wedding day.

We started telling friends. There wasn't going to be a formal reception. The house would be thrown open all day for friends who wanted to drop in. Excitement mounted by the hour.

What I hadn't taken into account, however, was Emma's reaction. She had been at Pat's when I told her the news. Three days later she returned home with some friends when Caroline was out. They raided the fridge, ate all the sausages and left the kitchen in a terrible mess.

Caroline was beside herself with rage again. It seemed she really hated the child.

'Thieving little bitch,' she yelled.

'How dare you talk like that about my daughter.'

We shouted at each other all night. Next morning the fox-fur muff was returned. The wedding was off.

Twelve

'Where are my fucking knickers? Emma's pinched my knickers again,' Caroline's voice screamed through the house.

'Daddy,' Emma flung herself at me, a picture of hurt innocence. 'Charlie hates me.'

It had become a madhouse with those two. Even Joanna, unable to stand the screaming matches, had moved out to share a flat. I would have left, too, but it was my house. One of them had to go.

It was July, almost at the height of a heavy London summer, and it was difficult to believe that in the January of that same year, Caroline and I had come within a few days of marriage. What held us together now was simply lack of courage to face life without each other. She had been part of mine for so long, yet it was impossible to continue the way we had become.

In Caroline's mind the girls had always stood between her happiness with me, and now she saw Emma as her rival. Both of them constantly competed for my attention. They were eaten up with jealousy about one another. Neither could accept that I loved them equally, if in different ways.

If Emma borrowed a record of Caroline's, ate some peanuts, pinched her knickers, Caroline flew into a rage. She even got angry just at the thought of what the child might have taken, even when Emma had taken nothing at all.

Emma was fifteen and had a boyfriend called Axel, a gentle, inoffensive Mexican of twenty-one, whose main fault was that he was lazy. Having come from a rich family, Axel didn't expect to have to work.

There was no harm in the boy. I considered myself lucky compared to what some fathers had to put up with. At least, my daughter had brought home a boy who didn't loll around and could string more than two words together, but because he was Emma's boyfriend, Axel didn't suit Caroline at all.

She could never use the phone because Emma was ringing Axel. She could never get into the drawing room because Emma and Axel were there, playing records, eating her peanuts, making a mess. Hadn't she warned me what would happen if I took Emma away from a decent school? The complaints were endless. There was never a moment's peace.

Caroline was not to blame. The two of them were as bad as each other. I had no illusions about Emma. to be. She really could bend the truth, and she could be devious to get her own way.

From leaving her first boarding school, she had become a weekly boarder at another, so she came home each week-end, but that still wasn't good enough for Emma. She behaved so atrociously at school that I was finally forced to put her in a day school, just round the corner from Launceston Place. Even that didn't totally satisfy her. She decided she wanted to come home for lunch. The excuse was that she could practise the piano at home. She loved the piano, or so she claimed.

It wasn't convenient. Caroline had a morning secretarial job with Robert Parrish, the film director, and it gave her extra work providing Emma's lunch. Directly the noise of piano playing started, Caroline bolted out of the kitchen and slammed the door furiously on her scales.

Emma had always been clever. Though ten years younger than Caroline, it was she who got the upper hand. Caroline was too straightforward to cope with her guile. While Caroline raged, Emma adopted her maddeningly cool, superior air.

'How dare you speak to me like that,' she'd say in haughty tones. 'This is my father's house, not yours.'

She struck Caroline at her most vulnerable point. She still had no claim on me, whereas Emma was my flesh and blood. If one of them had to go, Caroline knew who it would be.

Emma's behaviour angered me as much as Caroline's, but Emma was so much younger and still had a lot to learn. Caroline was the one who should have known better.

The summer got hotter. The atmosphere at home was as heavy as before a storm is due. I felt so much responsibility towards Caroline. If she was to leave, she was the one who had to decide it for herself.

As it happened, though, Emma left first. Pat agreed that she should stay with her for a while. That lasted six weeks, and then Pat decided to move out of London. Emma behaved badly at her mother's, who naturally blamed me. I wouldn't have put it past Pat to have Emma back. The one person who could break up my 'love-nest', as Pat put it, was Emma.

'If that fucking, devious little bitch comes back, I'm leaving,' Caroline yelled.

It always amazed me how Caroline could talk about people I loved in those terms. But I wasn't going to be blackmailed.

It was what Caroline had expected all along. All she felt about making a home for me and looking after my children poured out. After all she had done for me, I would always put my family first. That it wasn't that simple she could never accept. She was always saying I'd changed, but she also wasn't the girl I had once known.

Caroline stormed out of the room. From above came the sound of doors and drawers being slammed. Presumably she had started packing. There was nothing more to be said, so I got myself out of the way by taking Willy for a walk.

A removal van stood outside Launceston Place when I returned. Packing cases were being carted into the house. Caroline stood with a frozen expression in the hall, directing the cases downstairs to the dining room.

'What's all this about?' I asked.

'A lot of things in this house are mine,' she replied stiffly.

Somehow I hadn't expected anything as brutal as this. It reminded me of that last day at Ilchester Place. But if this was the way Caroline wanted it, I had no right to object.

The packing cases stood in a line along the dining-room wall. The white candlesticks had already disappeared. Caroline was in the kitchen, stripping it almost bare.

The kitchen was undeniably Caroline's. Whereas some women think of the bedroom as their domain, it was the kitchen where Caroline's character was expressed. Except for the fridge and the cooker, there was nothing in it from my past. She had chosen the pine dresser and table and chairs.

It wasn't any great shakes as a kitchen. There weren't many work surfaces, no flashy units at all. It was like a country-house kitchen, a homely place.

Caroline had always been a compulsive kitchen buyer. Gadgets of all kinds filled the cupboards and drawers, and it was those she was taking away. She removed most of the saucepans and casseroles as well. She was making sure life wasn't going to be easy when she left. There would be almost nothing in which to cook a meal.

She packed in total silence, and I didn't want her to leave that way. In fact, I didn't want her to leave at all.

'Will those chests be here for long?' I asked, as a means of breaking the ice. Also, there were so many, it would be impossible to use the dining room.

'Don't worry yourself. I wouldn't dream of cluttering up your life. They'll be gone tomorrow morning. I'm having them put into store until I find a place of my own.'

All this had happened so quickly that I hadn't even wondered if Caroline had anywhere to go. She announced that she was to stay at her ex-boyfriend's, as he already had friends living at the penthouse flat.

She gave me a look to see how I would react, but if she had expected jealousy, she was mistaken. My emotions were too numbed to feel anything like that.

'I'm glad you're going to a nice flat,' I said. Caroline marched out of the room with a toss of her head.

The last person she wanted around at that moment was me, but I couldn't leave her alone while she packed. I knew only too well what it felt like to leave a home.

All those heart-shaped bowls, porcelain dishes and little jewel cases disappeared from on top of the bedroom chest of drawers. Caroline dragged armfuls of clothes out of cupboards and drawers and heaped them into suitcases on the floor. She lost all her patience when she was in a mood, and, anyway, she never did know how to pack. Usually, I did it for her, but it wasn't the right moment for that.

Finally, her mother's photograph was laid on the top.

I glanced inside the cupboard to see if she had forgotten anything. A line of dresses remained. There was that cream wool Jaeger one, in which she was to have married, and which for ever after she had referred to mockingly as her wedding dress.

'I'll come back for those clothes later,' she said. 'I haven't got room for any more.'

The amount of packing cases downstairs could have held half the stuff in the house. But the last thing I wanted was an argument, and now the activity was over, Caroline's anger has dissipated. She was verging on tears.

The evening loomed in front of us like a threat. Left alone with her in the house, I would be bound to get sentimental and end up begging her to stay. The best thing was to go out.

We went to Annabel's, the Berkeley Square discothèque, which was not a good choice. Perhaps I took her there to get a little of my own back. Too often she had accused me of being too old to want to dance. But dancing means touching each other, and feeling Caroline's softness that night, it was so easy to be weak. Charles Aznavour's new record 'Dance in the Old-Fashioned Way' was being played. It was our favourite tune at that time, and too much for Caroline to take.

She was weeping as I hurried her out. We bumped into some friends just as we got outside the door. In the darkness they couldn't see Caroline's tears. When they asked us to stay, I agreed. I still wanted to hold that body of hers. It might have been for the last time.

We clung together in the darkness of the discothèque. She was everything again she had been that first evening we had danced together, and I watched the coloured ligths play in her golden hair. To part seemed impossible. yet so inevitable as well.

She didn't leave my arms until morning. In bed at home, we held on to each other all night. I stroked her hair.

'You deserve so much,' I whispered. 'I'm so sorry I've let you down.'

The silence I had always feared was there when Caroline left the house. Yet there was also balm in it. For too many years the houses I had lived in had vibrated with scenes. Silence didn't bother me any more, and as the day wore on I even welcomed it like a friend. It had become a peaceful house.

In my own mind, my relationship with Caroline was over. There was nothing we agreed about any more. Marriage was out of the question. However much we still felt for one another, we simply couldn't go on.

Yet Caroline had left the means to come back. There were those clothes of hers in the cupboard, the packing cases in the dining room, but, more important, there was also Willy, the dog.

Willy meant so much to Caroline. Sometimes, I even wondered if he was more important to her than I. In part, he was a substitute for the child I had denied her, but now I see that he meant more than that. Caroline needed love, and animals loved her. However much she got hurt, Willy's dumb devotion was always there. After a scene with me, she often buried her head in him, sobbing into his fur. Willy never let her down. She was certain to come back for him.

A day later, she phoned. The friends with whom she was staying were to be away that week-end. She didn't want to stay there on her own. If she could spend the week-end at Launceston Place, she promised not to get in my way.

She was out of her mind. The parting had hurt enough without having to endure another in less than a week. I had just started to adjust myself to her not being around.

She sounded furious. Didn't I owe her anything after taking four years of her life? Just the sound of her rage brought back a different atmosphere to the house. I had begun to enjoy being by myself.

Emma wasn't around that much, and when she was,

she was no longer any trouble. She kept the place tidy. She left the drawing room empty for me when I brought home friends. Emma triumphed over running the house, now Caroline was out of the way.

I kept busy myself. I went out a lot and brought home friends. I tasted a freedom I had never felt since I had married Pat. I could do what I wanted, go out and not wonder what trouble there would be in the house when I got back. Finally, I was learning to live with myself.

What was more difficult was going to an empty bed. It had been so long since I had slept alone. I hugged a pillow to help me to get to sleep and when I couldn't I sat at my desk and wrote the most appalling poetry all addressed to Caroline and all ending up in the waste-paper basket.

But in the small hours on one's own, thoughts and moods change quickly and quite irrationally.

Those clothes of Caroline's had become an irritation. It was as if she had left them in my bedroom daring me not to bring another woman back. I didn't want anyone else. I still felt too much for her for that, but I wasn't going to recover with constant reminders of her about the house. Willy had gone. Carol had taken him to the country for a bit.

Then little notes started to arrive. They could have been written in Caroline's tears. She woke in the night and reached out for me, but I was no longer there. She sobbed herself to sleep. It was so unnatural being apart. She didn't know who she was any more.

I could hardly bear to read those notes. I tore each one up. Even apart, we still tormented each other.

Then I became ill. Caroline got to hear about it and she phoned immediately. She had to come round; her place was at my side.

That was nonsense. She was the one who had walked out on me. If she was going to be emotional, I didn't want to see her. I didn't want to be vulnerable again.

But what with the notes, the phone calls and the clothes in my bedroom, something had to be done. Friends suggested I solved the problem by simply marrying her, but that seemed the last solution of all. I was determined to make the final break, so I sat up in bed and wrote Caroline a letter. It ended up twelve pages long. Much of it was historical facts, which we had been over together time and time again, but I thought she would understand clearly if it was set out on paper why it was impossible for us to carry on.

I explained how I had fallen in love with her quickly, too quickly perhaps, as she had seemed everything I had dreamed of, but no woman can be that,

I had told her all my sadness and my hopes, but I had made my love for my family perfectly clear. If she took me on, it was as a family man. Yet as far back as the Park Lane flat, Caroline had started to be jealous of my daughters. There was a scene when I had taken Joanna out to supper. Another when Pat was away from Ilchester Place, and I went home to spend a few hours with Emma so she wouldn't be in an empty house.

When we all lived at Lamont Road, there was so much trouble between the girls that I hadn't even wanted to move with them to Launceston Place, let alone marry Caroline and start another family.

I remembered a time when Emma was Caroline's greatest advocate. The sourness that had developed in their relationship had been started by Caroline. She wanted to be just with me and Emma stood in the way. Caroline couldn't share my love.

I didn't deny that Emma had been difficult, but she had a lot to learn. I was a proud father. I believed that with patience, understanding and kindness, Emma would grow up to be a splendid woman. But Caroline had lost Emma's respect.

Emma was the recurring theme in all our quarrels. She was the excuse for what was our own failure; it was

Caroline and I who couldn't get on. Though Caroline claimed to respect my principles, she disagreed with them. Respect with disagreement. That didn't sound good enough. Between the two of us there was no common ground.

Age and boredom had been thrown at me too often, as well as accusations about spending money I couldn't afford on my family.

I accepted it was boring for her knowing how successful I had been before, but I spoke of it only because I resented not being able to give much to Caroline. I had earned too much too early in my life. The timing was all wrong.

I told her how sorry I was to have given her so much unhappiness. 'You're always blaming me for taking your youth, and I do regret it,' I wrote. 'We both thought we could make each other happy and we have caused each other much pain.'

Caroline had asked me that if I didn't feel anything for her to tell her, so as not to prolong the suffering, but I did still feel for her, and she knew it. 'It's strange,' I said, as I finished the letter, 'that loving has got us where we are today – apart.'

It was a one-sided letter. It takes two people to ruin the relationship, but Caroline already knew my many faults. By telling her I couldn't change, I was sure she wouldn't want to go on.

Shortly after the letter was sent, a friend called Jean phoned. She had had a tearful Caroline to lunch. I wasn't surprised. I had wept myself, knowing I had ended everything between us.

'It's not like that at all,' Jean replied. 'Caroline knows how stupid she has been. She wants to try again.'

Then Caroline phoned. We arranged a dinner that evening at our favourite restaurant in Kensington, where the pianist used to play all the tunes we loved.

The food was awful, and Caroline's eyes looked even

more enormous in her pale, drawn face. I had lost eight pounds in weight in the six weeks we had been apart. But I was determined to hang on to my advantage. If Caroline came back, she was the one who had to accept I wasn't going to alter. Perhaps it was unfair of me, but it wasn't just love that held two people together. Ultimately, sharing the same principles was the strongest bond of all.

'Look,' I said, aware of Caroline's poor face, 'we both need a holiday, and I don't think I'll enjoy one without you.'

Pauline and James Guinness had invited me to their villa in the south of France. They knew Caroline well and wanted us to be together again.

Caroline moved back to Launceston Place that same night. Shortly afterwards, Emma moved into a flat. Then Caroline and I made a pact. It was then the end of August. If by 5 November we hadn't married, we would call it a day. We would have finally proved that we never would.

Thirteen

November 5th, 1974, came and went without either Caroline or me mentioning marriage. Even without Emma's presence in the house, we continued to have our ups and downs.

The longer a decision is put off, the harder it is to make. Caroline lived with me anyway. It was only a matter of popping around the corner to Kensington Registry Office and signing a marriage contract, but that seemed too simple for the significance marriage had for both of us.

Just as we'd always wanted to be the perfect couple, our wedding day had to be on a perfect day. But that's not easy to find in the everyday run of life. There was always some niggling problem, a letter from the bank manager, one of my stomach upsets or just another row.

Though Caroline and I got on better now the girls had left, we were still the same stubborn, strong-willed couple. Nothing between us had altered so drastically to make us certain marriage was the right thing.

Then a small tragedy happened in our lives. Smokey Jacobs, my Persian cat, died. To us, Smokey was one of the great cats of life. He had the most magnificent head.

Smokey was a travelling cat. He settled anywhere with me, though when we moved to Lamont Road I thought that we had finally lost him. After he had been missing for a day, I called the RSPCA. His habit was always to scout any new territory, but he had never been away that long. He was twelve years old, perhaps too old to have accepted the move, and had tried to find his way back to Ilchester Place. Two days later, though, Smokey had coolly walked in through the back door.

When he disappeared from Launceston Place, Caroline and I knew it was serious. Smokey was fourteen by that time, and lately he had grown terribly thin.

We had been having foul weather and when he went out, it rained heavily all night. Next morning, Caroline and I took either side of Launceston Place to search for him. I wrote cards to the whole street, asking people to look in their gardens for him. We knew he had gone to find a place to die.

It seemed hopeless. We had searched almost every front garden in the road. I had practically reached our front door when Caroline screamed on the other side of the road.

Before I could get across, she had climbed over the fence and got to him. Smokey lay under a bush, his coat sodden and bedraggled, but still with that magnificent head. He was almost dead, but he still managed to struggle violently when Caroline took him in her arms. He wanted to be left alone to die. He howled as we carried him to the vet.

The vet shaved a little patch on his leg to take the injection. Caroline clung to him so tightly she felt his heart stop. Her tears fell on his head.

The next morning I had to leave for Sheffield to do a radio show. I hated leaving Caroline when she was still upset. We had already lost Shaggy, the cairn. There was only Willy left.

Jean Rook, the newspaper columnist, was on the programme with me, and we travelled back together on the night sleeper to London. All my thoughts were with Caroline, and I started to tell Jean about her. I explained the reasons why I had never felt able to marry her.

'The vanity of men!' Jean exploded in her usual forth-right fashion. I should consider myself lucky to have a lovely young girl, who loved me and whom I loved. What amazed her was that I hadn't lost Caroline after keeping her waiting so long.

Jean talked about her own life. She had married late and had a small son. She didn't see any problem starting a family in middle age. There was more time for a child, and more experience of life to pass on. One wasn't so occupied with proving other things.

I reached home next morning when Caroline had already left for work. It was a clear, brisk day, so to recover from the stiffness of the night's journey I took Willy for a walk in Kensington Park.

I knew there had been a lot of truth in what Jean had said. There were often moments when I wished I was married again. I can't get married though, I thought, as I walked through the park: I didn't have a licence. Willy was pulling on his lead in the direction of Kensington Register Office. What fun it would be, when the right moment arrived, to ask Caroline to marry me, and immediately produce the marriage licence.

I walked into the registry office. 'How nice to see you, Mr Jacobs,' said the registrar. Caroline and I had met him together when we planned to marry the year before.

I told him that I had come to renew the licence. He got out my folder, which was out of date. I started filling in new forms.

'It is the same young lady, I presume?'

'Oh, good heavens, yes,' I replied.

Then I remembered I had come out without any money. It had started off as just a walk with the dog. But now I was in the mood, I wanted to get it fixed straight away. I promised to send the licence fee round by taxi.

The registrar told me a day's notice was needed to

get married. It was Monday; he suggested Wednesday. I thought he was rushing it a bit. 'Oh, I don't know about that,' I said.

Apparently, there was not much point renewing the licence without fixing the date. I wasn't doing anything on Wednesday. Neither was the registrar.

'How about eleven-thirty in the morning?' he asked.

Although it was unlikely that I would want to cancel it, to be on the safe side I asked how much notice I would have to give.

I just had to call him on Wednesday morning to call it off. Wasn't that awfully unfair? There might be some sweet young couple who wanted to marry at 11.30 on Wednesday morning, and my indecision would be holding them up.

'I've got no one who wants to marry on Wednesday,' the registrar replied. 'The morning is all yours.'

It seemed safe enough. I made the registrar promise, though, not to breathe a word to anyone.

I walked home slowly, wondering what on earth I had done. There was only one whole day left as an unmarried man.

I could take Caroline out to dinner that night. At the perfect moment, I'd say: 'What about marrying me on Wednesday?' I imagined the expression on her face.

Caroline didn't want to go out to dinner. She wanted to stay at home and wash her hair. Wasn't she always moaning that I didn't take her out enough? Finally, she agreed to come.

The restaurant was crowded. We waited twenty minutes for the table I had booked. During that time Caroline smoked three cigarettes.

'Do you have to smoke so much?' She promptly lit another one.

I decided to order some champagne. Caroline thought it a waste of money as she hadn't wanted to come anyway. She was right. She should have stayed at home and washed her hair. For once, it looked a mess.

The service was careless. The steaks were tough. Caroline insisted I had them sent back. She grew more irritable the hungrier she got. We were certain to have a row if we waited for another order to be cooked.

'It's not that bad.' I said, chewing violently on my meat. 'Be a dear and just eat it up.'

'For Christ's sake, when will you stop talking to me like a child?'

That finished it. When I got home I took the receipt for the licence straight out of my pocket and tore it up.

The next morning I had to leave early for Brighton to do a show. It was on my mind to cancel that blasted wedding when I got home that Tuesday evening. There was still plenty of time.

I walked through the front door at home at about five o'clock. Caroline sat on a chair in the drawing room, a large brandy in her hand.

'Any news? Any messages?' I asked.

There were apparently one or two. And a particularly interesting one on page five of the *Evening Standard*. I hadn't seen the evening papers. I had been reading a detective story on the train.

There was a photograph of Caroline in the paper. The story underneath it said that she was to marry me at Kensington Registry Office tomorrow.

It was a load of nonsense, Caroline had told friends and newspaper reporters who had constantly phoned. Then our journalist friend, Peter Noble, told her the press had got the news from the registry office itself. So Caroline phoned the registrar. When she found out the truth, she was in a flaming mood.

The least I could have done was talk to her about it. Didn't I think a girl likes to know when she's going to get married? It wasn't only men who were allowed to change their mind about that sort of thing. She made me sound like the last man she'd ever marry.

I couldn't understand why she was so cross. After all, I had proved I wanted to marry her. I would have gone through with it, too, if the previous evening she hadn't been in such a filthy mood.

We had a dreadful row. Then we went out to dinner with friends and hardly spoke at all. There was definitely not going to be a wedding.

Directly we got home, she went upstairs to the spare room and slammed the door. I could hear her sobs.

By four o'clock that morning, the occasional sob from the spare room told me she was also awake. The situation was absurd. 'Look,' I said, standing in the doorway. 'I have heard of some ridiculous things in my life, but for a girl to leave the bed of the man she's been living with for years simply because he decided to marry her seems potty to me.'

Caroline smiled. She came into my arms. She was softness again. Why didn't we go ahead and marry the next day?

She had nothing to wear. But that wasn't important. It was to Caroline: she'd never been married before.

'I want to know when I'm going to do it,' she said. So that was that.

Next morning, she looked so miserable as she left on her bicycle for work. It could have been her wedding day.

Newspaper reporters and photographers with telescopic lenses had gathered outside by the time I left the house.

'Let's take a picture of the groom,' one shouted.

'You can take my picture if you like, but all I'm doing is going out to lunch,' I replied.

Of course none of them believed me. I had a lunch date, and a procession of press cars followed me all the way to the restaurant.

Fourteen

The top button of my new, plain blue shirt flew off and Mr Lawrence, a valet with impeccable references from Windsor Castle, whom I had employed for the day, sewed it on with black cotton. With the house in such confusion, it was the only colour I could find.

Downstairs, Mr Beard, our regular butler at parties, polished champagne glasses in a drawing room alive with the scent and colour of dozens of flowers.

It was 12 March 1975, our wedding day, and nothing on earth would have stopped me marrying Caroline this time. Going about it the wrong way two months before had proved one thing to Caroline. After all those years, she suddenly realized that I really meant to marry her, if only she stopped trying to prove I never would.

There was no need to push me any more, to test feelings she no longer doubted. When uncertainty disappeared, so did Caroline's moods. She became herself, and that was the girl I wanted to marry. So sure was she of me that even the fact that a date wasn't fixed didn't bother her. She left me to get around to it in my own time, and once she did that, I couldn't wait.

It seemed absurd to feel so wildly excited about marrying a girl who had already shared nearly six years of my life and had lived with me for the past four. Just signing a marriage licence had always seemed too easy a way of changing anything, but now I knew Caroline was right. It did.

Marriage was the trust between us. It meant that we were no longer afraid of where loving each other might lead. We had tested the feeling for each other so often, yet it had survived. Now it would grow even stronger in the security of Caroline being my wife.

We were determined to do everything properly on our wedding day. I had a new, dark grey, chalk-striped suit, a new shirt and plain, blue tie. Caroline was a copy-book bride – something old, something new....

She wanted to have a blessing from the Bishop of Crediton, a family friend, and a rabbi, after we had been married. Caroline was accustomed to going to church on special occasions. She was afraid she wouldn't feel properly married in just a room.

I was in the drawing room by eleven o'clock, waiting for Caroline. It was, in fact, another Wednesday, the same day we always picked to get married. The time was also the same as on those two previous occasions when we hadn't made it. It was almost as if the Kensington registrar left each Wednesday at 11.30 a.m. free, while he waited for Caroline and me to get round to the inevitable.

Mark George, one of Joanna's friends, had already arrived, and he poured a glass of champagne. I watched my hand tremble as he held it. I hadn't expected nerves as well.

I was desperate to get through the ceremony. There was so much I had to tell Caroline, words I should have said years before. It would have been unbearable if anything went wrong now.

Why was she taking so long? Girls got cold feet as well as men. All I had seen of her that morning was a streak of blonde hair, dashing from one room to the next. Did she still doubt me, even though I had no doubts left?

It took a moment to realize she was there. There was such stillness about her as she stood on the stairs in a cream silk dress. It was a plain dress, rather like the first wedding dress she had bought, except this time there was no red fox-fur hat. Just her hair, which hung to her shoulders and framed her face, as it was in all my fantasies.

She was dressed so simply, but she was luminous all the same. Her skin glowed with everything she felt.

Caroline had a wedding present for me. It was a signet ring, engraved with the Munro family crest. Then it was my turn to give mine. I had replaced the leather frame around her mother's photograph with a silver one.

If my present had been diamonds or pearls, Caroline would have been thrilled, kissed me excitedly and then shut the box. This present was too much: she couldn't accept it without tears.

I grabbed her arm and rushed her out of the house. A maroon Rolls-Royce, which belonged to a friend, waited outside. His mother's silver-blue one had also been lent for us to make the five minutes' journey from the registry office.

Inevitably, the press had discovered that we were to make another attempt at marriage, and they weren't disappointed this time. Flashbulbs popped again, and reporters shouted questions as we flung ourselves into the back seat of the car.

Our wedding meant too much to us, and we wanted to keep it a personal moment. Just a few close friends were at the ceremony. David Merrion Williams, husband of Caroline's cousin, Wendy, and her friend, Tanya, were the witnesses. Emma and Joanna were there.

The drab chilly register office room we had feared turned out to be a room of flowers, with traces of confetti and rice, and an atmosphere that came from all the hopes of couples who had stood there before us.

Caroline and I signed the register. It was the moment

when I was expected to kiss my wife. I looked into her face. The flush of nervousness had disappeared, but Caroline's skin still glowed.

As we had always planned, we didn't have a formal reception. It wasn't even a family affair. Johnny and Patricia Munro didn't come, as we would visit them in Cornwall the following week-end.

Friends started dropping in as soon as we got home. Dick and Caroline were there. They had been married before us. Dick and I both made it after all.

A photographer from the *Daily Mail* phoned to ask if he could take pictures at the reception. Caroline hadn't wanted the press to know about our wedding, but now she was actually married, it was different. She invited the photographer at once. She even started to worry when he was late. It was as if she suddenly wanted to share her happiness with everyone.

Six o'clock came and the drawing room was still packed. Mr Lawrence and Mr Beard had been pouring champagne constantly since mid-day. Caroline and I had a long drive to the Manor House Hotel at Castle Coombe, and I wanted to take my wife away.

When we finally left, Willy was in the back of the car. Not even a honeymoon would have been quite complete without the dog. Julian Marshall, who had been Jeremy's room-mate at school, rushed towards the car as we drove down Launceston Place. He carried a bunch of flowers for Caroline.

The hotel receptionist greeted us with eyebrows slightly raised. The bridal suite must have seemed an odd choice, when we had often stayed at the hotel as Mr and Mrs Jacobs before. I didn't care what anyone thought. Even if it was only one night, I was determined to have a proper honeymoon.

We had more champagne at dinner, sent by her cousins, Wendy and David, and Caroline's head started to nod. It was definitely time for bed. I lay on the four-poster and Willy stretched out on a rug, as she disappeared to the bathroom to get undressed. I was glad she was behaving coyly. It was as exciting as if we had never been to bed together before.

She had never taken so long about it either. Eventually Willy gave up and fell asleep. I couldn't think what was taking her so long. Finally, she appeared. She wore a long, white nightdress which was so delicious it stayed on for less than a minute.

I felt more romantic that night than I had ever felt before. I found myself saying what a terrible fellow I had been, but I swore that I'd make it all up to Caroline. I heard myself declaring my undying love in a way that would have done justice to the talents of Laurence Olivier in *Wuthering Heights*. Never had I thought it possible to feel so much for anyone before.

Caroline smiled contentedly, but she seemed at a loss for words.

Next morning, no one expected to see us come downstairs for breakfast. The story of the wedding was in the newspapers, and honeymooners usually spend their first morning in bed. What those hotel guests didn't realize was that we had been having breakfast together for years.

Caroline immediately ordered black coffee. She had a hangover.

'I don't remember a thing about last night,' she said. 'Did I get to bed all right?'

From Castle Coombe, we drove to Bristol for the weekly recording of 'Any Answers'. The honeymoon was over, but it was still a special time. A reporter from the local newspaper interviewed us. As Caroline talked to him, I thought of that first night we had spent together in Bristol, when it had seemed impossible ever to marry Caroline. Now she was answering questions as my wife.

The next day we travelled to Exmouth where 'Any Questions' was being broadcast.

Edward du Cann, the Tory MP, was on the team that week, and after dinner his wife Sally leant across the table with a packet of cigarettes.

'Would you like a cigarette, Mrs Jacobs? Mrs Jacobs, Mrs Jacobs . . . Mrs Jacobs. . . .

Silence fell. Everyone waited for the moment when Caroline would recognize her new name.

At last, it clicked. 'Oh, you mean me!' she cried.

We headed down the Exeter bypass towards Cornwall to spend the week-end with Caroline's parents. It was a trip we had made many times before, but everything seemed to have more meaning now.

'I don't know why, but being married does feel different,' Caroline said.

'It's a nice feeling.'

Just as she spoke, a car flashed across our path. We were travelling fast, and I slammed the brakes and swerved violently to avoid it. When we finally pulled up beside the kerb, shaken and pale, the road was totally clear. The other car was nowhere in sight. It was as if it had never happened. The car had appeared from nowhere and then vanished. It seemed almost like a ghost.

Caroline pushed a loaded wire trolley across Launceston Place. The supermarket around the corner allowed her to take the shopping home in it as she was pregnant. I hurried down the front steps. I hated Caroline carrying anything, and my anxiety amused her, when I was hardly new to fatherhood.

Everything that happened with Caroline felt different now. It was more than just starting again. For example, when we walked in Richmond Park with Willy, she would walk alongside me, whereas before she always walked ahead, alone, a habit from her childhood. Patricia and Johnny had noticed that, too, when we had been with them in Cornwall.

A letter addressed to Mrs Jacobs waited on the console table in the hall. Caroline picked it up and laughed. It still tickled both of us when she was called by her new name.

Why hadn't I married her years before? That was a question that was later to torment me. But it wouldn't have worked before. Caroline's view of marriage was too romantic and mine too cynical. We both had had a lot to learn before we bridged that gap.

Now we enjoyed the sweetness of being newly married, without the problems of getting to know one another as well. All the pieces had fallen into place. Caroline had even become close to Emma and Joanna again, now she was expecting her own child.

'Where's that wicked step-mother of mine?' Emma shouted whenever she visited home. Caroline introduced both girls as her step-daughters. It was a running joke between the three of them.

I wheeled the emptied wire basket to the supermarket and hurried home. Caroline was curled up in her usual position on the green sofa. She had become a thoroughly expectant mother. Even though she was only three months' pregnant, she already looked the part. Her stomach swelled in readiness for the growing child, and her breasts were large and full. She made everyone feel she was the first woman ever to have a baby by the awed, excited way in which she talked.

I remembered the slim, almost flat-chested girl I had first met. Her body had quickly rounded when she fell in love with me. It became voluptuous and soft. Emotions always changed her shape.

She took my hand and placed it on her stomach to feel the baby. It was a daily ritual with us, although at that stage there was really nothing to feel.

I always had a little chat with him as well, telling

him not to expect some young energetic father but a worn-out old dad.

'I never did get that wheelchair catalogue,' said Caroline.

'But I'll give you another couple of years yet.'

We had already named the child Ben. We couldn't think of any girls' names, probably because we hoped it would be a boy.

What school did Caroline want to send him to? We had better put his name down directly he was born. Her son go away to boarding school! She couldn't bear the thought. In so many ways, Caroline had changed. She still glanced through 'William Hickey', but now she also read *The Times*.

Just being at home together put me in a cosy mood. I started to talk about decorating the nursery. We had already chosen Emma's old bedroom as the baby's room. But Caroline was superstitious about such plans. When Tanya had given her a baby's rattle, she was quite upset. She thought it unlucky to buy anything for the child before it was born, and, besides, there was still plenty of time.

She switched on the television. 'Crossroads', her favourite serial, was on. She never missed an episode. There were still one or two subjects Caroline and I disagreed about.

Johnny and Patricia Munro came to stay with us and Caroline became even more radiant than ever before, her happiness at their staying in our home knew no bounds, she completely redecorated the top bedroom especially for them. She'd never painted anything before and she completed it in a day. We took them to our favourite play – the musical version of *The Good Companions* at Her Majesty's Theatre. How Johnny cheered at the end and how they loved having drinks afterwards with John

Mills in his dressing room. He still reminds me that we were the only couple who had seen his show four times and paid for our seats on each occasion. He's wrong, we saw it five times.

We gave a party for Caroline's parents when they were in London, and two friends of theirs called Gordon and Gladys Symondson came along.

Gordon was an architect, and he talked about the holiday villa he had built in Spain. A large living room stretched right across the top of the house, with views that looked out across the Spanish hills to the sea at Fuengirola. It had a large garden, full of purple bougain-villaea flowers and fig trees, which surrounded a swimming pool.

Gladys joined in the conversation with her strident Dutch-English voice. The house was standing idle. Why didn't we use it for a holiday?

It was an idea. This was the end of June, and Caroline and I still hadn't made any plans. Perhaps Dick and Caroline would join us. It sounded marvellous to them.

The first three weeks in September were fixed, and as the time approached the two Carolines were constantly on the phone. Their excitement spilled over Dick and me. We even started phoning each other, asking what clothes we were going to take.

But there was still some time to go and 'Any Questions' wasn't quite ready to take its summer break. Almost at the end of the season it was broadcast from Tain in the North of Scotland and one of my dear friends, the actress Liz Ashley, invited us to stay in her lovely house nearby, a converted crofter's cottage on an estate belonging to Arthur Munro-Ferguson. Liz's husband Richard Matthews had to return to London for a television play, so it was just Liz, Caroline and me and, of course, Willy. Most things to Liz are 'total magic', but her relationship with Caroline was even more so, it was as if she had found the daughter she had never had. They were inseparable.

We walked, we toured but most of all we laughed and laughed. Liz gave dinner parties and we were invited with her to others.

It was as if by magic that we dined with Captain Patrick Munro of Foulis, the head of the Munro clan. Caroline sat at his right hand and mentioned that, as a Munro herself, she had given me on our wedding day a ring with their crest on it – was it the right one? After inspection he suggested that she look at the crest on the plates in front of us – they were the same. She mentioned a near relative who had held high office in New Zealand. The head of the clan opened a book and found the name not far removed from his own. The former Miss Munro glowed with pride. Her day was made.

Back in London just before we left for Spain we gave a party in the garden of Launceston Place. We drank champagne, and the summer flowers that Caroline had planted scented the dark, warm air.

The party was Caroline's idea. She said it would be a long time before she would see her friends again.

Fifteen

I woke on the tenth day of the holiday in Spain to a strangely silent house. Normally Dick, an early riser, could be heard pottering about, but that morning everything was still. A water sprinkler outside hissed over the damp, sweet-smelling grass.

Caroline lay beside me, sleeping quietly. A line of startling white sunlight edged the curtains. Another perfect day. The weather was so good, it was almost boring. Not a cloud ever interrupted the brilliant blue of an endless sky.

I was glad Dick was still in bed. Since our hosts, the Symondsons, had left the villa three days before, he and Caroline had moved into their bedroom. They had such a small room before, with such small beds, that Dick's 6 ft 4 in. frame had to curl up to fit into bed.

Now they were comfortable in a room more spacious than ours, with their own bathroom. It was a green bathroom, such a nice green, too.

I stretched out in a room warm and musty with garden scents of bougainvillaea flowers and ripened figs, and I looked at Caroline. One of life's great joys was still to watch her sleep, surrounded by all that hair of hers. I moved her head gently to see the changing effects. It didn't disturb her. She slept as peacefully as a child.

She had looked incredible in a long, red dress when we

visited the Marbella Club. As usual, the place was packed with well-known beauties – who paraded with their sleek, brown bodies, manes of luxurious hair and contrived faces. To my mind, they had looked like strutting peahens against the naturalness of Caroline.

A friend of ours suggested I should have her portrait painted. Caroline had never looked so lovely, now she was to have a child. Pregnancy had changed her. It was Caroline who was the first to suggest that the two girls sunbathed topless at the villa. It wouldn't have surprised me if the other Caroline had decided to do it, as she was a great girl for nudity, but my Caroline had always been a bit of a prude. So natural was she about it, however, that soon the rest of us were plunging completely nude into the swimming pool.

Caroline was growing up. Her twenty-ninth birthday would be in September, the same day as we returned home from Spain. Almost too old for me I would have thought, if she'd been that age when I first met her. But in those six years I had grown up as well.

My birthday present to her was wrapped up at home. She hadn't wanted me to bring it to Spain, as she wouldn't have been able to resist opening it before the day. It was a strand of pearls, the longest I could afford. I remembered that little pearl necklace Caroline had worn the first night I had seen her. She hadn't changed for me. She was still my tweeds and twinset girl.

Caroline stirred in the bed. She moved her head about the pillow, like a contented cat.

'What's the weather like?'

'Pouring.'

'Twitface,' she smiled.

What an idle creature she was, lying there as if she had nothing better to do all day. A mammoth shopping expedition in Fuengirola had been planned. The four of us had spent the previous evening discussing all the delicious food we would buy.

Caroline continued to smile. The sunlight glowed on her pillow, and she moved her head gently in it, feeling its warmth. The white rays touched the edges of her hair.

I was drawn to her by the completeness of just being together. It was sweet making love in the morning sun. All I felt was in that moment. The four of us being alone in the house . . . the long, lazy days, filled with nothing but sunbathing and swimming, good food and elaborate plans for little expeditions which we made . . . and laughter, often hysterical laughter, that came from the true friendship we four shared.

We had all been through a lot to reach this moment in our lives. We were ready to enjoy it.

Caroline and I were seldom morning lovers, but as I left her, I thought of all those mornings when we would make love again.

She called me from the bathroom. It was time to feel the baby. Caroline was five months' pregnant, but she still looked much more than that.

I stroked the roundness of her body. 'I hope everything's all right at Launcey Place,' Caroline said. That was her nickname for home. As much as she enjoyed the holiday, Caroline was becoming nesty. She almost wanted to go back.

The day before we had been driving together in the Spanish hills. The Mediterranean glittered behind us, and, in front, hill rolled into hill to become the Pyrénées. We faced north. I only had to keep driving and in a couple of days we would have been outside the house.

Why not? We could do anything now. There was no one to hurt any more. No one to worry about but ourselves. We could plan endless tomorrows together.

The idea of driving home appealed to Caroline, but we finally decided against it. 'We can always do it another time,' she said.

I made breakfast that morning. Toast and eggs. Then

a quick swim before we took the winding, dusty track which led down from the villa to the main road. The small market town of Fuengirola was about two miles distant, marked on the horizon by a strip of blue sea.

Modern, whitewashed villas stood out on the pale rouge-coloured hillsides, surrounded by lush groves of fig trees. How piggishly we had all eaten those figs at the start of the holiday, until Caroline had bitten one which bulged with maggots. She screamed and screamed. She was terrified the maggots would get into her body and harm the baby. We all roared with laughter at such an idea, but I noticed that not one of us touched another fig after that.

It was to be barbecue night at the villa. It was the same almost every night. Dick was our 'barbecue king'. We sat in the garden, sipping red plonk under a violet sky, while he cooked sausages and chops on an open fire. It was to be fish tonight.

The Fuengirola market was a modern, grey-stone building, cool and antiseptic against the dusty heat outside. The noise and smells had an excitement, though, and Caroline dashed from stall to stall as usual, buying far too much.

Fish with weird shapes and of vast size lay with staring glassy eyes and blood-red guts on the cold, stone slabs. We bought red mullet for supper. Tomatoes, sweet onions, pimentos, peaches, vivid in their Mediterranean colours, quickly filled two large shopping bags.

The sunlight was dazzling as we stepped outside. Holidaymakers in bright, skimpy summer clothes and silly hats pushed past tubby Spanish women, dressed in black, and working men with buttoned-up shirts, ill-fitting suits and complexions swarthy from the sun.

Caroline wore a little white dress with shoulder straps and a pattern of beige flowers. The sun was in her hair and glistened on her skin. It seemed to me, in my romantic mood, that the crowd stepped aside to let her pass. She looked such a golden girl.

The two girls wanted to go to another shop. Caroline started running across the road. She shouldn't dash about in her condition. If anything happened to the baby, I didn't know what she would do.

Dick's eyes were also fixed on his Caroline.

I said to him, 'It's amazing to be so happy. I've never felt so marvellous in my life.'

'I feel like a seventeen-year-old boy,' Dick replied.

Dick and Caroline wanted to see the beach to find out what we were missing in the hills. Caroline and I had seen it before, so we waited while the other two took a stroll.

We perched up on a wall beside a row of cafés advertising everything with chips and English tea. An old couple sauntered past us, hand in hand. They must have been in their seventies, and it was obvious they were English, as the man carried a folded copy of the *Daily Express* under his arm. He was quite a bit shorter than his wife, who was a cosy, pear-shaped woman with thick legs, and wavy, old-fashioned hair. He sported a bushy military moustache.

Their dignified clothes looked odd beside the briefly clad holidaymakers who swarmed around. I guessed they were an ex-colonial couple who had lived a lot in hot countries and covered up to avoid the sun.

'Aren't they sweet?' murmured Caroline. 'They could be us one day.'

It was a nice thought, if an impossible one. I would always be that much older than Caroline. When she was their age, I wouldn't even need a wheelchair. I just woudn't be around.

'Hasn't it ever occurred to you that I might go first?' Caroline asked.

We only had four minutes left together, but there was

no warning in her voice. She made the remark in such an ordinary way.

Dick and Caroline came back. How right we had been. The beach was frightful, with sunbathers packed as close as sardines. Wouldn't they be envious of our cool villa and private swimming pool?

We piled into the car. Dick was in the front passenger seat to accommodate his lengthy legs, the two girls in the back. I always drove. It had simply happened that way when we picked up the hired Fiat at the start of the holiday. I don't think Dick much liked to drive.

There was a yacht basin at the end of the promenade, and I gazed longingly at the luxury of the boats. I wouldn't have minded having one of those.

'Another day,' said Caroline.

I had to get moving. Everyone was starving hungry. All the food was in the boot, it was almost mid-day. Soon we would have lunch.

The main road from Fuengirola to Málaga was one I hated. I already knew it, as I had often had holidays in Spain with Pat. It was a twisting, turning racetrack, sometimes as wide as a dual carriageway, at others nearly as narrow as a single track.

Caroline loathed it, too. It had upset her when we had driven past the bodies of dogs, hit by uncaring drivers in a mad dash towards the sea. I had passed dead dogs like that in Israel, on the journey to Jeremy's funeral. No one had bothered about them there, either. Their bodies rotted under the sun.

We approached the left-hand turning to the small road, which led up to the villa.

'Right ho, Chairman!' I said to Dick. That was a favourite nickname of mine for him. 'Preparing to move into the centre lane.' I sounded like a pilot in touch with ground control.

'Road clear . . . arm going out . . . nothing coming behind. . . .'

It was impossible to miss the turning. The spot was a famous landmark, as a sprawling white farmhouse stood on the corner, with directions to Fuengirola and Algeciras painted in large, uneven letters on the outside wall.

Gladys had warned me about the dangers of that turning. She suggested pulling into a lay-by opposite to wait until the road was clear. I had even tried it once or twice, but the road was never clear. One way or another, cars belted along – and pulling into lay-bys seemed no way to drive.

I stopped the car in the outside lane for a few seconds, its indicators flashing to the left. Two police motor-cyclists approached from the opposite direction, travel-ling fast and floating in the shimmering heat. Their roar fled past us. The road fell silent again as I pre-pared to make the turn.

The noise when the van hit us from behind was ear-splitting. It stunned me for a moment, and then I realized that the car was travelling through the air.

Trees and sky passed, but with such breathtaking slow-ness that inside the small car, it felt as if the four of us were suspended in time.

What a nuisance if the car was mucked up. It would be such a waste of the holiday going through the business of hiring another one.

I looked across at Dick. As if in slow motion, his body rose in an arch from the seat, and then sank back again. Then I saw blood pouring out of the corner of his mouth.

The car travelled through the air, then crashed back on to the road, coming to rest yards onwards. Instantly, I looked behind to see what had happened to Caroline.

Her hair was spread across the back of Dick's seat. It fell around her face, just as it always did when she fell asleep. It was Caroline's face, but somehow it wasn't her any more. The warmth had gone.

She was asleep, that was all. Shocked, unconscious, even. Nothing serious. There wasn't a mark on her. She couldn't be badly hurt. Dick's Caroline looked exactly the same. She was asleep as well. What I couldn't understand, though, was my Caroline's foot was next to her face.

The baby! I had completely forgotten about the child. I must get Caroline out of the car. The impact wouldn't have done it any good at all.

I opened my door and rushed round to the back. There was nothing left of it. The car's boot had been squashed right into the back seat.

I wrenched at the door next to Caroline's seat. The metal was twisted and crumpled as if it had been squeezed in someone's hand.

Dick dragged himself out of the front seat. Then he collapsed by the roadside, his mouth pouring blood. The sight of the blood stunned me. I let go of the door and started running up and down the road. I heard myself screaming and the screams of others, too. Cars had stopped bumper to bumper along the road. Complete strangers were crying out with shock at what they saw.

Not one of them knew Caroline was pregnant. I had to tell them. Someone had to get her out of that car.

The two police motor-cyclists who had passed while we waited at the junction returned when they heard the crash. They wrenched open the door on the other Caroline's side, and they lifted her out. Would no one help my Caroline?

'My wife . . . my wife . . . she's pregnant,' I yelled, as I ran up and down the road. I couldn't seem to stop.

A man grabbed me by the arm. He was a Swedish journalist, I later learned. 'Don't worry, your wife's got a very badly broken leg, that's all.'

That stopped me running. Hadn't I seen Caroline's foot next to her face? I had to believe him. That was all I could bear to hear.

Blood poured down my left leg, and I looked at it as if it was someone else's blood. The hand with which I touched my face was bloodstained, too. It was swollen, but I felt no pain.

I stood calmly beside the car and watched as Caroline was carried away from me.

It didn't make sense. I had always wanted to die in Caroline's arms. It would have been easy in her warmth. Now her body was being lifted into the ambulance. I could have gone to see it, but I didn't. It didn't even occur to me to say good-bye.

There was no need. Caroline had already gone.

Sixteen

What happened afterwards I will always remember as the most savage and brutal experience of my life.

The two Carolines were taken in the ambulance to Málaga hospital. Another ambulance arrived to take Dick, who was obviously in a worse state than me, to a first-aid station at Fuengirola.

I was left beside the crumpled car. A policeman handed me Caroline's Gucci handbag, stained with blood. Blood poured down my face. My left arm was numb. It was becoming almost unbearable to stand on my left leg.

Twenty minutes passed and no ambulance arrived. Cars were still in an endless traffic jam down the road and strangers gaped at me.

The two police motor-cyclists persuaded a Spaniard, who had pulled up at the crash, to drive me to the first-aid centre in his car.

Persuaded is too mild a word. The Spaniard protested violently. He gesticulated, shouted, even screamed about doing it. He had no wish to be landed with a swollen, bleeding foreigner who might even die in his car.

He was still in a dreadful state when we drove off. He shouted at me in incomprehensible Spanish. I shouted back that Caroline was pregnant. Someone had to be made to understand that. If the girl lost her baby, what would she do?

An ambulance appeared, travelling in the opposite direction. The Spaniard jammed on the brakes, and with arms flailing wildly, flagged it down.

I tried to explain to the ambulance driver about Caroline but he just shook his head.

I was limping badly by the time I walked through the first-aid centre. Mothers clutching children on their laps and old ladies in black stared as I passed. I judged from their shocked expressions how I looked.

There was a small room with two beds, and on one of them lay Dick's enormous bulk. He was an awful mess as well. He was shouting for his Caroline.

A nun came in. She spoke to us in Spanish, but she calmed us both with her voice.

A man in white overalls appeared. He was a burly chap with thick, black eyebrows and a shock of black hair. Carefully, he cut away the sleeve of my shirt.

It was my favourite shirt, a brown one, which I had bought ten years before at John Michael in the King's Road. It was worn and faded, but I liked the familiarity of old clothes. I had on a pair of white shorts that day.

My arm was an incredible sight. It swelled into every colour of the rainbow as well, but there was still no pain.

The swarthy fellow fetched a board shaped like a boomerang. He placed it under my arm, then covered it with yards of bandage and wads of cotton wool. Then he dressed the wound on my left leg.

The two of us were wheeled into another ambulance to go to Málaga hospital, which was where our wives had gone.

Those thirty miles were a nightmare. The ambulance driver appeared just as anxious to get rid of us as the Spaniard who had been landed with me in his car. What made the journey worse was that Spanish drivers don't give priority to an ambulance. No one bothered to get out of the way as we hurtled passed.

Dick and I were thrown about as the ambulance skidded round corners, mounted pavements and each time it crashed back on the road, Dick screamed in pain. He lay on a stetcher, while I sat in a small seat, and blood poured from his mouth. I was terrified that he was about to die. He thought his lung was punctured. I kept assuring him he had only lost some teeth, though I had no idea what was causing so much blood.

I was in a strange state. Pain came and went, as if it was still only the fear of pain I felt.

Dick repeated again and again, 'Please let my Caroline live.'

'She's all right,' I said. 'There wasn't a mark on her. And Charlie's okay, too. She's got a broken leg, that's all.'

We were wheeled into a corridor at Málaga hospital, where a line of injured people waited for treatment. They were accident cases as well, people with damaged limbs, bleeding hands and injured eyes, and they moaned with pain.

We stopped each nurse and white-suited doctor that passed. What had happened to our Carolines? No one spoke English. No one knew where they were.

A doctor arrived, accompanied by a pretty young girl in a dark blue dress. 'Don't worry. Don't worry,' he said in a heavy accent, 'she speak English.' He pushed the girl towards us.

'Good afternoon,' she said.

At last, someone to help us. The questions tumbled out. How were our wives? Did they know my Caroline was pregnant? How soon before we saw them?

'Good afternoon,' repeated the girl. Those were the only two words of English that she knew.

Eventually Dick and I were taken to treatment rooms. I was examined by a doctor and then wheeled into an operating room where four young men in stained white suits waited for me. Two were smoking; another pinched a nurse's bottom as she brushed passed him. Then they bent over me with garlic heavy on their breath.

The four young men stitched up the wound in my leg without giving me an anaesthetic or a tranquillizer, and then they set my broken arm in plaster. While they worked on me, I talked to kill the pain. I tried to explain who Dick was. If someone knew that, we might get help. The young men repeated the last word of all my sentences as they stitched me up. They didn't understand a single one.

At last the British Consul arrived. He told me that both our wives were still in surgery. What had confused the hospital was that both women were called Caroline.

Dick was also still being treated. The Spanish hospital discovered he had two broken ribs. The X-ray machines in Spain could not be noted for their accuracy: when he arrived home, it was found that Dick had seven more ribs broken as well. Fortunately, though, he hadn't punctured a lung. He had just badly bitten the inside of his lip.

I waited alone in a small room. How I longed for something to drink. We hadn't had one since breakfast time. I would have given anything for a cup of tea.

Dick was sitting in a wheelchair, surrounded by several doctors in white suits. I was wheeled in front of him. By his expression I knew the moment had come. 'Well, old lad,' he said. 'I've got to tell you. Your Caroline is dead.'

I could hear myself howling. Jeremy. Now Caroline. A son. A wife. Both killed on foreign roads. It wasn't possible. It wasn't fair. . . .

Dick's Caroline had brain injuries. She too wasn't likely to survive.

I was wheeled out of the room and down to the reception desk. Caroline's father was on the phone. The police in Cornwall had been contacted directly Caroline's identity had been discovered. Johnny Munro had known about her death almost at the same moment as I had been told. What could I say to him?

'How are you, old cock?' Johnny's voice shook slightly, as he tried to sound his usual, friendly self. He had lost his only daughter, and the one chance he'd ever have of becoming a grandfather, yet there was concern in his voice for me.

The British Consul suggested Dick and I would be more comfortable in a nursing home. Anywhere would have been better than that hospital, so once again I was loaded into another ambulance by excited, gesticulating Spaniards. I only travelled two hundred yards. The nursing home faced the hospital. At the gate, a porter demanded money before he would let me in.

I fumbled in Caroline's bag and found £20. That wasn't enough. Money wasn't a problem, I assured him, but my assurances weren't enough.

Twenty minutes passed before the Consul arrived with Dick. We were admitted to the nursing home, where we were put in a twin-bedded room. Then we were left alone.

A crucifix hung over my head. Dick said that the 'Star of David' would have been more appropriate. Somehow, we managed our first laugh.

We were both desperate for a drink, but no one appeared to give us anything. At last a doctor arrived; he read our reports and gave us both an injection to make us sleep. We begged for a bottle of water.

Dick and I made a pact that night. When he cried, I didn't. I filled in the gaps. Neither of us slept at all.

Next morning, the door opened and a handsome young man with sun-blond hair strode in.

'David!' he declared. 'I can't tell you how sorry I am.'

I recognized him as a journalist on one of the popular dailies; but I couldn't quite place where we had met.

'I do hope you'll give the story to us.'

Dick was so badly injured that he needed two strong

men to lift him up in bed, yet he still found the strength to leap at that journalist. He collapsed in agony as the young man ran from the room.

The world's press waited outside. Photographers trained long-range lenses on our window as they perched in the trees nearby.

Some friends on holiday in Spain arrived. The owner of a restaurant near our villa, where Caroline and I had often dined, came to help us. He became our interpreter at the clinic.

I stayed there one day more because I didn't want to leave Dick. But then I had to get home; there was so much to be done. So I left Dick alone. The Spanish restaurateur put me on the plane.

Johnny had left Cornwall at dawn to be at London airport in time to meet me. With Wendy and David he took me home to Launceston Place and Carol, Joanna and Emma.

Seventeen

The house looked exactly as we had left it, and that seemed unreal. It was as if I had stepped back on to a stage set when the play was over and I had no part in it any more.

Her possessions were around me. The porcelain bowls and heart-shaped dishes stood on the chest of drawers. Her mother gazed out from the new silver frame. Caroline's perfume lingered in her clothes. The plants and shrubs, which she had planted in the garden, still grew.

It seemed that she had just popped out to get the shopping. I started each time I heard someone at the front door. She would be back soon. She had always come back before.

The days passed, and gradually I realized that she would never return to me. Perhaps she had never existed at all. She was always the golden girl of my fantasies, and now she felt like a dream. If only I could wake up from this nightmare.

But the accident had happened. Every stab of pain, the aching of my injured, swollen body told me that and, at the height of pain, I cried out for Caroline. I clung to my pillow and, in the night, I called her name. She had cried to her mother. Why wouldn't Caroline help me now?

My body began to recover. I returned to work. Another series of 'Any Questions' started. The only way was to cling to what was left.

Numbness took the place of pain. So much emotion had carried me through the funeral, giving her possessions away. Now the house was still. Only emptiness remained.

I still had something that belonged to Caroline, which had never been hers. I took off the coloured wrapping paper around her birthday present. The pearls glowed like her skin, but she had never seen them, worn them around her neck. There was no emotion when I returned them to the jeweller's shop.

I got home to find a small cheque for an insurance policy on Caroline's life. I stared at it. What could I do with such a payment? As I stood in the hall, I noticed the stair carpet was frayed. It had always irritated Caroline. She would like a new one.

It was different when I lay in bed that night. I cried but the nightmare was over, and when I called Caroline's name it was softly, because I could feel a wisp of her hair on my cheek. I knew that if I could bear not to touch her, she would never leave me again.

Each night in bed, I found her there, and she was in the daytime, too. If I heard a joke, I could laugh again, because I knew how Caroline would laugh, and it seemed as if we could still laugh together, too.

At the roadside landmark on a farmhouse wall in Spain, Caroline had left behind her body, but not her love. We still shared that. She was still my wife. I knew that was true because I felt it, but there was no logic in it, and I could not see how it was so.

That was why, with Sue's help, I decided to retrace the journey of our life together. This book is the result. It has helped me to understand.

God bless you, darling Caroline.

The Author

David Jacobs has been a broadcaster since the age of eighteen. He has worked on many popular television and radio programmes, including 'What's My Line', 'Housewives' Choice', 'Juke Box Jury' and 'Any Questions' which he is currently presenting. In 1960 he was voted BBC Television Personality of the Year, and he was voted BBC Radio Personality of the Year in 1975.

David Jacobs has been Chairman of the Stars Organization for Spastics and Vice Chairman of the RSPCA. He published his autobiography, *Jacobs' Ladder*, in 1963. 1963.

THE DISTANT SUMMER

Sarah Patterson

Kate was seventeen, restless, eager to explore the world that lay beyond the walls of her father's Norfolk rectory.

Johnny was the young tail-gunner on a Lancaster bomber – bitter, haunted, searching feverishly for peace between nerve-tearing bombing raids over Germany.

As the summer wore on and the bombing missions were stepped up, they had to learn to live – and love – facing the terrible possibility that next time Johnny might not come back . . .

'A moving story beautifully told' *Daily Mirror*

ANOTHER BREATH OF BORDER AIR
Lavinia Derwent

'Looking back, I often wonder if any of it was real . . .'

Lavinia Derwent, well known as a best-selling author of children's books and as a television personality, here memorably portrays a childhood spent on a lonely farm in the Scottish Border country.

Hers was an enchanted world of adventure: a world of wayward but endearing farm animals, and of local characters like Jock-the-herd . . . and Lavinia's closest friend, Jessie, who never failed to temper her earthy wisdom with a rare sense of humour.

'A love of a book' *Glasgow Herald*

THE NEXT HORIZON

Chris Bonington

A successful expedition to the summit of Annapurna; a hair-raising trip down the Blue Nile; a visit to Hunza, the remote country buried in a Himalayan valley – this is the world of Chris Bonington, climber and adventure journalist.

This book is an extraordinary record of Chris Bonington's development as a climber and as a man.

If you would like a complete list of Arrow books please send a postcard to
P.O. Box 29, Douglas, Isle of Man, Great Britain.